Cross-Cultural and Religious Critiques of Informed Consent

This book explores the challenges of informed consent in medical intervention and research ethics, considering the global reality of multiculturalism and religious diversity. Even though informed consent is a gold standard in research ethics, its theoretical foundation is based on the conception of individual subjects making autonomous decisions. There is a need to reconsider autonomy as relational—where family members, community and religious leaders can play an important part in the consent process. The volume re-evaluates informed consent in multicultural contexts and features perspectives from Buddhism, Confucianism, Hinduism, Christianity, Judaism and Islam. It is valuable reading for scholars interested in bioethics, healthcare ethics, research ethics, comparative religions, theology, human rights, law and sociology.

Joseph Tham is Full Professor in the School of Bioethics at Ateneo Pontificio Regina Apostolorum in Rome, Italy.

Alberto García Gómez is Chairholder, UNESCO Chair in Bioethics and Human Rights, and Professor in the School of Bioethics at Ateneo Pontificio Regina Apostolorum in Rome, Italy.

Mirko Daniel Garasic is a researcher at LUMSA University and Adjunct Professor of Bioethics at LUISS University in Rome, Italy.

Routledge Focus on Religion

American Babylon
Christianity and Democracy Before and After Trump
Philip S. Gorski

Avantgarde Art and Radical Material Theology
A Manifesto
Petra Carlsson Redell

Pandemic, Ecology and Theology
Perspectives on COVID-19
Edited by Alexander J. B. Hampton

Trump and History
Protestant Reactions to 'Make America Great Again'
Matthew Rowley

Theology and Climate Change
Paul Tyson

Religion and Euroscepticism in Brexit Britain
Ekaterina Kolpinskaya and Stuart Fox

Owning the Secular
Religious Symbols, Culture Wars, Western Fragility
Matt Sheedy

Cross-Cultural and Religious Critiques of Informed Consent
*Edited by Joseph Tham, Alberto García Gómez,
and Mirko Daniel Garasic*

For more information about this series, please visit: www.routledge.com/Routledge-Focus-on-Religion/book-series/RFR

Cross-Cultural and Religious Critiques of Informed Consent

Edited by Joseph Tham,
Alberto García Gómez, and
Mirko Daniel Garasic

LONDON AND NEW YORK

First published 2022
by Routledge
2 Park Square, Milton Park, Abingdon, Oxon OX14 4RN

and by Routledge
605 Third Avenue, New York, NY 10158

Routledge is an imprint of the Taylor & Francis Group, an informa business

© 2022 selection and editorial matter, Joseph Tham, Alberto García Gómez, and Mirko Daniel Garasic; individual chapters, the contributors

The right of Joseph Tham, Alberto García Gómez, and Mirko Daniel Garasic to be identified as the author of the editorial material, and of the authors for their individual chapters, has been asserted in accordance with sections 77 and 78 of the Copyright, Designs and Patents Act 1988.

The Open Access version of this book, available at www.taylorfrancis.com, has been made available under a Creative Commons Attribution-Non Commercial-No Derivatives 4.0 license.

Trademark notice: Product or corporate names may be trademarks or registered trademarks, and are used only for identification and explanation without intent to infringe.

British Library Cataloguing-in-Publication Data
A catalogue record for this book is available from the British Library

Library of Congress Cataloging-in-Publication Data
A catalog record for this book has been requested

ISBN: 978-1-032-07313-2 (hbk)
ISBN: 978-1-032-12094-2 (pbk)
ISBN: 978-1-003-21321-5 (ebk)

DOI: 10.4324/9781003213215

Typeset in Times New Roman
by Apex CoVantage, LLC

The UNESCO Chair in Bioethics and Human Rights (www.unescobiochair.org) organized a workshop on "Bioethics, Multiculturalism and Religion" and the papers submitted here form the collection of this edited volume.

This UNESCO Chair was established in 2009 with two Roman universities. It offers a university framework of reflection and study, providing information and fostering the application of bioethical principles in science, medicine and new technologies based on the Universal Declaration on Bioethics and Human Rights. Through integral education, research and information, it seeks to contribute towards the recognition and promotion of a global and integral vision of bioethics, bringing to light universal values and principles as well as social and legal implications in relation to human rights. By creating a community of persons who are interested in these values, it seeks to promote cultural dialogue and encounters in a spirit of solidarity.

This book has been elaborated under the EU project i-CONSENT (https://i-consentproject.eu) that has received funding from the European Union's Horizon 2020 research and innovation programme under grant agreement No. 741856.

Contents

List of contributors   ix

Introduction   1
JOSEPH THAM

PART I
Multiculturalism and relational autonomy   9

1 **Ethical issues concerning informed consent in translational/clinical research and vaccination**   11
   ALBERTO GARCÍA AND MIRKO GARASIC

2 **Informed consent and minors in a multicultural society**   18
   MIRKO DANIEL GARASIC AND FABIO MACIOCE

3 **Community engagement in the informed consent process in global clinical research: international recommendations and guidelines**   31
   MARGHERITA DAVERIO

4 **Healthcare decision-making: cross-cultural analysis of the shift from the autonomous to the relational self**   44
   JOSEPH THAM AND MARIE CATHERINE LETENDRE

PART II
Religious perspectives on informed consent 57

5 Informed consent: a critical response from a Buddhist perspective 59
ELLEN Y. ZHANG

6 A Confucian view of informed consent in biomedical practice 71
RUIPING FAN

7 Hindu norms on human experimentation: parsing classical texts 79
JOHN LUNSTROTH

8 Informed consent and clinical trials: a Jewish perspective 97
DAVID HEYD

9 Christian perspectives on informed consent 105
LAURA PALAZZANI

10 Fitting informed consent onto an Islamic moral landscape and within Muslim contexts 116
AASIM I. PADELA

Index 128

Contributors

Margherita Daverio is a research fellow at LUMSA University and Assistant Professor in the *Master in Global Bioethics* online (Universidad Anáhuac, México).

Ruiping Fan is Professor of Philosophy in the Department of Public Policy at the City University of Hong Kong.

Mirko Daniel Garasic is a researcher at LUMSA University and Adjunct Professor of Bioethics at LUISS University in Rome, Italy.

Alberto García Gómez is Chairholder, UNESCO Chair in Bioethics and Human Rights, and Professor in the School of Bioethics at Ateneo Pontificio Regina Apostolorum in Rome, Italy.

David Heyd is the Chaim Perelman Professor of Philosophy at the Hebrew University of Jerusalem.

Marie-Catherine Letendre is founding member of Bioethics International, Inc.

John Lunstroth is a fellow of the UNESCO Chair in Bioethics and Human Rights and a lecturer in the Medicine & Society Program at the University of Houston.

Fabio Macioce is Full Professor of Philosophy of Law and Bioethics at LUMSA University, School of Law, Rome.

Aasim I. Padela is Professor and Vice Chair of Research and Scholarship, Department of Emergency Medicine, and Professor of Bioethics and Medical Humanities, Institute of Health & Equity, The Medical College of Wisconsin, Milwaukee.

Laura Palazzani is Professor of Philosophy of Law at LUMSA University in Rome.

Joseph Tham is Full Professor in the School of Bioethics at Ateneo Pontificio Regina Apostolorum in Rome, Italy.

Ellen Y. Zhang is Professor of Department of Religion and Philosophy, Hong Kong Baptist University, Hong Kong.

Introduction

Joseph Tham

Informed consent is a gold standard in Western medicine. There are nuances to its application under diverse contexts, be they in public health, clinical research or the bedside. Since the 1960s, the backbone of informed consent in research has been firmly enshrined. Its formulation and justification have evolved since the Nuremberg code and the Universal Declaration of Human Rights. In medical research, we can find guidelines on informed consent in numerous international documents including, for instance, the Belmont Report (1978), Council of Europe's Oviedo Convention (1997), The Universal Declaration on the Human Genome and Human Rights (1997) and constant updates from Council for International Organizations of Medical Sciences (CIOMS), the World Medical Association's Declaration of Helsinki and the UNESCO Declaration on Bioethics and Human Rights (2006).

Despite the general acceptance and practice of informed consent in medical intervention and research ethics, there are still challenges to overcome and concerns that need further evaluation. For instance, informed consent needs to be tailored to the individual and is a process rather than a formality. The ways to communicate, present information will, therefore, depend on the literacy and cultural context of the subjects and patients. A genuinely informed decision needs to be free and enlightened, and a simple signature is not enough. There must be a trusting relationship between the patient and the physician–researcher who, at the same time, must consider the vulnerability of being someone who is ill and in need. We must address the false hopes and desires of participating in trials that may or may not be curative. There is a greater awareness of the exercise of autonomy in vulnerable groups of subjects such as volunteers, children, migrants and ethnic minorities. We need to consider the communitarian nature of decision-making in many cultures.

As a Research and Innovation program (2014–2020) of the European Union, Horizon 2020 funded the i-CONSENT consortium to improve the information that patients receive from clinical research by creating

DOI: 10.4324/9781003213215-1

personalized and innovative informed consent.[1] Being a partner in this venture, the UNESCO Chair in Bioethics and Human Rights investigated "the ethical gaps, barriers and challenges currently present in obtaining informed consent in biomedical research, prior to the administration of vaccines, and during translational/clinical vaccine research involving human participants."[2] Within this project, the UNESCO Chair has a particular focus on the multicultural and interdisciplinary dimension of informed consent. This volume, therefore, collects the papers generated from i-Consent as well as other related articles.

Together with some of the i-Consent partners, the UNESCO Chair held its 6th International Bioethics, Multiculturalism and Religion Workshop on the topic of Informed Consent on 21–23 February 2018. Bioethical and religious scholars from Buddhism, Confucianism, Hinduism, Christianity, Judaism and Islam came to Rome to discuss the key challenges and the requirements of informed consent in clinical research. They identified some of the challenges present in obtaining informed consent from patients/subjects in different, challenging cultural contexts representing minority groups and vulnerable populations.

Multiculturalism and relational autonomy

The first section of this book collects four articles on the topic of informed consent in cross-cultural contexts. In these essays and reports, there is an unease with the overtly individualistic conception of autonomy that undergirds the process of informed consent championed in Western medicine. The process of obtaining consent in different cultures, minors, family dynamics and community settings may require more than a straightforward signature of the patients or their proxies. These different situations mean that an overemphasis on individual rights and autonomy might be detrimental to truly informed consent. The articles evince the need to consider autonomy as relational—where family members, community and other stakeholders can play an essential part in the consent process.

Already in the report generated for the Horizon 2020, i-Consent project has a section that focuses on how multicultural background can influence informed consent. The challenges regard the prospective patients' ability to fully understand the disclosed information as well as the procedural barriers that prevent them from giving genuinely informed consent. It discovers that there is a need to examine cultural and social variables when assessing the ethical validity of this consent process because a monolithic, individual-centred version of autonomy in the Western contexts may not be congenial to vulnerable migrants or cultural groups. The report recommends a new look at "communal" and "relational" autonomy where deliberation and legitimacy of a decision not only belong to a single person but involves the community—such as the family—to which the subject belongs.[3]

The first chapter from Garcia and Garasic looks at informed consent from the angle of human rights and mental privacy. Advances in biotechnology and neuroscience propitiate the need to consider additional rights that protect cognitive liberty, mental privacy, mental integrity and psychological continuity. These new requirements will have implications for informed consent in the context of religious diversity.

Garasic and Macioce's chapter on "Informed Consent and Minors in a Multicultural Society" looks at the unique needs of minors who cannot give full, independent and competent consent as they are not yet grown-ups. In cross-cultural and multi-religious settings, this legal age distinction can create additional problems of interpreting individual autonomy. The case of the underaged minors calls for an adaptation of the notion of self-determination to include relational autonomy.

Daverio's chapter on "Community engagement in the informed consent process in global clinical research: international recommendations and guidelines" delineates how informed consent in global clinical research will require engagement with the community. This involvement in collaborative research will need further analysis and formulation of ethical goals and guidelines towards meaningful participatory processes. The author discusses the main strategies for community involvement in research settings internationally and the steps to work towards a more relational view of the self.

Finally, Tham and Letendre confront the cultural shift of individual to relational self in the West and the implications of decision-making and informed consent in healthcare. The article traces the history of Western medicine from "paternalism" to autonomy in the physician–patient relationship as a result of rapid advances in medicine. Due to different historical and legal demands, patients became gradually more involved in the decision-making process. Nevertheless, it soon became apparent that informed consent may turn out to be a procedural or legal requirement that does not holistically embrace all the patient's situation. To correct this imbalance, they observe in the literature a more nuanced shift from the individual to the relational self where a richer conception of moral agency is emerging.

Religious traditions on informed consent

In the second section of the book are the papers submitted to the workshop in Rome by the six major world religions and their cultural ambits.

According to Zhang, Buddhism does not have any canonical norms on most bioethical topics, which are Western constructs. Buddhism would allow for the rights language of informed consent to protect the individual agency, truth disclosure and self-determination in healthcare decisions. However, the Buddhist tradition is wary of any individualist notion of a substantial self as someone who can make real free choices. Since ontological selfhood is elusive, any exaltation of autonomy would be problematic. The Buddhist vision of interdependence sees absolute self-determination as untenable since we cannot fully define the self except in relation to others. Buddhists consider that we are predetermined and conditioned socially, and karmic causality is at work without our knowledge. As Zhang says:

> In the case of informed consent, it is very often difficult for physicians (as well as for patients) to determine if a patient's deferral of decision-making is his/her own choice or the result of formative influences of the family. It follows that the patient's capacity for intentional action is also questionable. Voluntariness involves the idea of "free will," which would be problematic for Buddhists, and medical decision-making based entirely on patient-centered orientation would be problematic for Buddhists as well.

According to Ruiping Fan, Confucian ethics is based on virtues rather than on rights, liberty and equality so prominent in Western ethical systems. However, Confucianism will accept legitimate human rights that protect individual interests to enhance virtuous living. Fan thinks that neo-Confucianism can accept minimalist rights developed along the lines of Rawls that would include the right to life, security, liberty, conscience and equality before the law. However, these are not to be conflated with full-fledged individual rights understood in the West. Confucian China considers medicine as the art of *ren* or benevolence. In this understanding, the training of the physician is meritocratic and virtue-based. Patients implicitly trust the benevolence of their doctors, and informed consent is, therefore, absent in this relationship. Fan claims,

> Chinese physicians must have gained consent, either explicitly or implicitly, from patients and their families in order to conduct medical treatment, but it is also clear that obtaining such consent before treatment has never been formally and clearly required in the tradition.

Besides, Confucianism emphasizes shared family decision-making in healthcare, which can come into conflict with the liberal understanding of autonomy. At the same time, the patients prefer to involve family members in making healthcare decisions, which does not necessarily mean medical paternalism. Instead, it implies that Confucian patients can autonomously accept familism as the best choice to make these decisions. Autonomy and self-determination are not part of the Confucian virtue-based ethical system.

Lunstroth looks at the classical texts of "Hinduism" for the grounding of consent in research. India is a secular state that accepts biomedical ethics, despite being Western constructs, as a political structure to protect the vulnerable. Since Hindu ethics is only relevant to the householder stage of life, which is of the political order guided by *dharma* as order, law or duties, only the *Arthasastra* of *Kautilya* contains a systematic theory of political/legal order. This text can offer insight into the *dharma* of the scientific enterprise and the role of informed consent. As such, Hinduism evaluates research ethics through the ethos of sacrifice.

Lunstroth is highly critical of the current arrangement, where a subject often becomes a data point for the sake of scientific advances. There is a commodification of human bodies as tools to be exploited. Benefits for the future generations are also not evident, as the results of the research are often oriented to commercial benefits or privatized as intellectual property. The research subjects are sacrificed and do not receive the benefits for themselves or for their community, and they cannot readily negotiate or sue the researchers. As Lunstroth comments,

> The emphasis of the rule on the sacrifice being completed suggests the state is interested in maintaining the integrity of the sacrificial transaction . . . the drug company sacrifices the individuals who "consent" to participate. The company strips value from them, aggregates and then monetizes it for itself. The god is the neoliberal economic system that awards greed, and the sacrifice usually works.

Hence, in the context of the *Arthasastra*, informed consent in research is an impure sacrifice since the research subject is often ignorant, the researchers and industry are somewhat corrupt and the political order is too compromised to protect its citizens.

We now turn to the monotheistic religions. The Jewish discussion of informed consent relied on rabbinical sources, according to David Heyd. The underlying question deals with the question of whether one can sacrifice physically to help or save someone else. This tradition seeks a balance between self-preservation and self-care, and the supererogatory social commitment to promote the public good. Contemporary rabbinic opinion on informed consent holds that doctors need to consult patients or family before they enter experimental trials. There is also a presumptive force for the doctor to safeguard the patient's life. While Judaism accepts the practice of informed consent, it rejects its theoretical basis of autonomy since God alone is sovereign over our lives or our bodily parts. Heyd explains,

> The requirement of consent in medical treatment is based on the potential suffering and harm to the body and on the duty of self-care rather than on the idea of the absolute control of human beings over their lives. Thus, informed consent is not a major principle in the doctor-patient relationship, since there is a duty of the doctor to heal and a parallel duty of the patient to be healed. Being cured is not a matter of choice or of personal autonomy.

Akin to Muslim practices, Judaism allows for "different amounts of information to different subjects based on their individual degree of anxiety." Finally, informed consent depends more on legitimacy—mediated through the rabbis—than on individual autonomy.

Laura Palazzani recognizes that informed consent in research, as practised in the West, is compatible with the Christian worldview. The values of human rights, dignity, respect for privacy, freedom to decide, justice, risk and benefits, beneficence and non-maleficence found in the secular framework resonates with the Christian ethical framework. However, Palazzani notes that Christianity derives these bioethical principles from the concepts of God's creation, human finitude, imago Dei, our ability to know the truth and act according to it and the infinite value of human life and its eternal destiny. The dignity of human life also implies the possible choice to sacrifice oneself in research out of charity and solidarity. It is a laudable act for the benefit of the common good. Hence, Palazzani believes that informed consent is:

> inspired by Jesus, who cured the sick *with compassion, generosity, and understanding*. Christians believe that disease and suffering are trials from God to bring them closer to salvation through death and into His grace. Scientific research should be done for the purpose of serving those who are ill, not solely or primarily for the benefit of the researchers.

Nevertheless, there are also aspects of informed consent that might diverge from the secular approach. The protection of vulnerable groups due to the severity of the illness, age, gender, socio-cultural conditions must also extend to the most fragile member of the human family—the human embryo and foetus. Hence, research done on them is highly contentious. The Christian and mainly Catholic understanding of human sexuality precludes involvement with specific techniques of contraception or assisted reproductive technologies, especially if they could harm the embryos. On certain occasions, the physicians and researchers should have recourse to conscientious objection to abstain from participating in some acts which, as stated before, are essential values for Christian living where objective truth and salvation are at stake.

Padela shows in his chapter that Islamic moral theology will support aspects of informed consent although it would not ground this ethically from the principle of respect for autonomy. Instead, something equivalent to the basis of informed consent will come from Islamic theology of moral liability in front of God. Moral liability (*taklīf*) means standing before God in judgement and being morally responsible for one's actions. For Islamic bioethics, every action has moral significance, and patients need to properly consider both the mundane and afterlife ramifications of participating in medical research. Hence, informed consent processes can aid Islamic individuals to live morally.

Islamic theology aside, Muslim states and culture are also varied, according to Padela. Many of them have pronounced communitarian ethos, with responsibilities of medical decision-making residing in the broader community. Padela writes,

> In many Muslim societies the patient-doctor dyad is often not the only locus of decision-making. . . . People trust their relatives and community members and value interdependence, therefore limiting decision-making within person-centric rights can deny the value attached to such relationships.

Muslim patients do not expect or desire a great deal of explicit information. Paradoxically, too much information can leave them to feel uninformed and can even generate distrust. Moreover, Muslim societies need to ground ethics regulations within Islamic law. For instance, Saudi laws make repeated references to the *Sharia* as a source of guidance on research ethics.

The inadequacy of the autonomous self

These chapters have shown that many religious traditions challenge the Western idealization of the autonomous self. They prefer a more relational or communitarian understanding of doctor–patient or researcher–subject relationship. Western medicine and its current gold standard of informed consent may not adequately address the theoretical scepticism by different religions and cultures towards its underlying grounding of autonomy.

As these chapters have shown, Eastern religions are more sceptical of the bioethical discourse based on human rights while the monotheistic religions are more compatible with the informed consent discourse.[4] Despite external similarities and acceptance of informed consent at a practical level, there are deep theoretical and foundational problems. The concept of the self in different religions can explain how these difficulties arise.[5] In Eastern cultures, selfhood is illusory or derives meaning through interdependence with nature, family or community. This understanding can pose a challenge to the atomic self from which informed consent is derived. Western monotheistic religions define self-identity with a transcendent God. They tend to be more legalistic in their approach and derive legitimacy from the scriptures or religious authority. In all the religions, the language of sacrifice is prominent in the framework of research ethics, where the patients act virtuously in solidarity for the greater good of fellow humans. Informed consent points not only to earthly existence but also to the less tangible questions of life, be they in the imperceivably small embryos or that of the mysterious afterlife.

From a practical point of view, these differences in the foundational values are becoming more pronounced with migration and increased affirmations of cultural groups when they participate in clinical research. A swift from individual to relational autonomy may be more consonant with the greater research populace who tend to frame healthcare decisions and understanding of illness and well-being in religious terms. Embracing these ideas can offer a more nuanced improvement of the readability, design and obtaining process of consent. As different chapters in this book show, this shift will better align the conscious and unconscious cultural biases of the investigators with the multicultural and religious variables of the subjects. This shift can proffer a cross-cultural vision of vulnerability that can enhance knowledge, communication and empathy in consent to research. Consequently, more individualized approaches will help frame multi-layered informed consent which includes these global perspectives.

Notes

1 This book has been elaborated under the EU project i-CONSENT (https://i-consentproject.eu) that has received funding from the European Union's Horizon 2020 research and innovation program under grant agreement No. 741856.
2 The full report can be accessed here: https://i-consentproject.eu/wp-content/uploads/2019/01/D1.4-Ethical-issues-concerning-informed-consent-in-translationalclinical-research-and-vaccination.pdf.
3 *Ibid.*
4 See J. Tham, K.M. Kwan, and A. García (eds.), *Religious Perspectives on Human Rights and Bioethics* (Dordrecht, Netherlands: Springer, 2017).
5 See J. Tham, C. Durante, and A. García Gómez (eds.), *Mind, Genes and Self: Religious Reflections on the Impact of Emerging Technologies on Human Identity* (Abingdon, UK: Routledge, 2018).

Part I
Multiculturalism and relational autonomy

1 Ethical issues concerning informed consent in translational/clinical research and vaccination

Alberto García and Mirko Garasic

Improving the health literacy of patients in relation to medical practices and research is essential for upholding the principle of respect for autonomy—that is, respecting the patient's ability to make self-governed choices regarding medical interventions or research participation that reflects the patient's beliefs and values.

This report[1] provides a full review of informed consent challenges (i.e. ethical gaps, barriers and priority needs) that are unique to certain vulnerable groups, namely, preadolescents, adolescents, and pregnant women, with a specific emphasis on how neurobioethical, multicultural and interreligious variables should be taken into account when assessing the appropriateness of the current documents relying on the notion of informed consent. In exploring how we are to improve the process of obtaining informed consent, we will also highlight the relevance of bias and privacy in the debate. The objective is to offer recommendations on how these gaps, barriers and challenges may be solved or avoided in the future.

There are two categories of challenges. The first category comprises challenges that are patient-centred, which prevent a research subject from fully comprehending the disclosed information. The second category comprises challenges that are process-centred, which are procedural barriers that prevent obtaining truly informed consent from prospective patients.

The types of recommendations explored for solving or avoiding these two forms of barriers in the context of research and vaccine administration include: 1) understanding more in depth the potential information derived from progress in neuroscience; 2) taking into account the role of religion and non-Western cultures in relation to a person-centred way of conceptualizing informed consent; 3) improving the readability and design of consent forms; 4) identifying the cultural and other bias of both the patient and the doctor/researcher; 5) evaluating the role of privacy in the collection of sensitive data connected to informed consent; 6) incorporating education-specific strategies to improve patients' or participants' understanding of

DOI: 10.4324/9781003213215-3

consent information; 7) initiating discussion of meningitis, HPV or RSV immunization and clearly explaining the benefits of infection prevention through immunization; 8) inviting questions at every step of the consent process; 9) acknowledging and addressing discrimination based on age and gender; 10) obtaining consent from legal representatives (in the case of children or pregnant women limited by mental defects or disorders); 11) protecting the privacy of participants enrolled in vaccine-related research; 12) acknowledging patients' or participants' own experiences with meningitis, RSV and/or HPV infection; 13) implementing procedures to assess patients' or participants' capacity to consent; 14) supporting parenting strategies and lifestyle practices that reduce and reverse predisposing risk factors to meningitis, RSV and HPV infection; 15) adopting individualized approaches to promote health protective behaviours (tailoring the consent process to reduce concerns relating to vaccine cost, pain, safety, side effects, perceived appropriateness to lifestyle and/or need for multiple doses) and 16) implementing a dynamic informed consent model with participant control, accompanied by appropriate privacy safeguards.

A multicultural and interreligious perspective on informed consent

The UNESCO International Bioethics Committee stressed in more than one occasion that an individual has to be informed as much as possible on the outcomes of the procedure in which she is involved in:

> The close connection between autonomy and responsibility supposes that consent be freely given by the person concerned, the clearest possible information be provided, his/her faculties of comprehension be intact, that he/she has been able to assess the consequences of participating in a research project and the development of the entire process, as well as fully understanding the advantages and disadvantages of possible alternatives, also in terms of treatment.[2]

Aside from this analysis, various cultural and social variables are to be considered when assessing the ethical validity of the informed consent process. Oftentimes, such considerations might impinge upon the monolithic, individual-centred version of autonomy that we tend to give for granted in the Western contexts, creating a space for new versions of vulnerability—in which the vulnerable population is represented by those individuals unable to see their attitude and perception of autonomy as sufficiently represented by current legislations. In some scenarios, for example, we could use "communal autonomy" or "relational autonomy," a version of autonomy that sees the deliberation and the legitimacy of a decision to belong not only to a single person but rather the community to which one belongs (i.e. family). Often leaders of the community—nearly always family members—are those who make the decisions and their judgement is not questioned due to their age, expected wisdom and knowledge of the community's internal dynamics in place.

Individual and relational autonomy

In line with what just described, the words of Joseph Tham and Marie Letendre are particularly relevant to understand more accurately how some of our standard ways of conceptualizing the discussion around informed consent might not be as given as expected.

> Cultural norms specify behavior. 'Honesty is an ideal value for most Americans, but it varies in strength as a real value for other cultures.'[3] Honor is highly prized in the Japanese culture as is female purity in the Islamic world. Direct eye contact is avoided in several cultures, notably Asian and the Middle Eastern culture; the Navaho use silence to formulate their thoughts in order to give the most complete answer. Trust is given only to family members in the Gypsy culture. Masculine and feminine pronouns do not exist in Asian languages, and 'yes' does not always mean the affirmative since many cultures use the 'yes' as a way of avoiding an embarrassing 'no'. This is just a short list of cultural variables that inform and form communication styles. A cross-cultural health care ethic combines the tenets of patient—family centered care with an understanding of the social and cultural influences that affect the quality of medical services and treatment. Developing sensitivity to different cultures can make health care programs and activities attractive and interesting for a broader population base. In contrast, a lack of cultural sensitivity can deter people from using health care services.[4]

Hence, not all documents that assume that focusing on the individual might be sufficiently sensitive towards how one person with a cultural, religious or identitarian background might want (or is capable) to express her views, values and desires if disconnected from her community. In accepting this reality, it is equally important to bear in mind, as Loredana Persampieri rightly stresses, that—though contemplated—relational autonomy has no effective role in the shaping of informed consent in official forms.[5]

Seeking consent from an individual is necessary, even if the community is consulted, but the actual value of the consent of such individual, once the community has given its approval or disapproval, often raises concern. Nevertheless, such reasons should not lead to the conclusion that cultural considerations pave the way to situations where, exceptionally, for members of some groups communal autonomy may override individual autonomy. Conversely, we should always bear in mind that "respect for cultural diversity and pluralism should not be used to infringe fundamental freedoms nor any of the principles set out in the Declaration."[6] In this perspective, the Italian National Bioethics Committee suggests an interpretation of the concept of autonomy in terms of "relational autonomy," which may be better tailored to an intercultural approach aimed at accommodating the value of the community dimension in certain cultural settings (i.e. African tribes) and respect for the person.[7]

As the notion of informed consent relies on a set value of individual autonomy that not all cultures and approaches to life share, a patient's cultural disposition and past experiences with medical healthcare professionals will have an impact on the amount of trust that they can have in a vaccines' efficacy, for example. Although local culture may shape people's perception over time, people are more likely to trust experts that share a similar background, tradition, religion and culture with them.[8] When working with ethnic minority patients, it is important to note that comprehension may also transcend simply linguistic barriers. The conceptualization of illness and cultural bias both plays a role in the ways that information is presented and understood. Thus, it is important to understand the role that culture plays in obtaining informed consent.[9] In particular, in multicultural societies, where a large portion of the society is made up of immigrants with varying cultural backgrounds, there may be differing attitudes regarding the role of physicians. Moreover, the quality of informed consent may be dependent on the relationship between a physician and their patient.

To improve the physician–patient relationship and for the consent gained to be effective, there has to be a partnership based on openness, trust and good communication between the two parties.[10] Individual's religious beliefs or related cultural values can lead to questions and concerns that health professionals, unfamiliar with the religion or culture, have not encountered before. It has been shown that culture (which can also include religious and spiritual backgrounds) can impact one's vulnerability to infectious diseases. Rejecting treatments or prevention measures due to religious or cultural values is not a new phenomenon; there have been reports of vaccines-preventable outbreaks in religious schools, congregations and religious communities.[11] As a case study, the World Health Organization reported that in a region in Nigeria 16% of the children were vaccinated against polio. The reason for the low vaccination rates is that the community is predominantly Muslim, and they believe that the polio drops are used as a tool to sterilize the children. Likewise, a study from the Netherlands has shown that municipalities with high orthodox protestant domination have lower vaccination rates compared to municipalities without an orthodox protestant domination.[12]

Regarding the way informed consent notion interacts with biomedical research, some of the key questions that we want to address here are:

a) How much of the notion of informed consent is applied in one's tradition? And in which way?
b) Can or should we have different informed consent forms for differently vulnerable populations?
c) Do all traditions agree with the general principles behind informed consent (i.e. the prioritization of individual autonomy)? If not, what alternative values/approach could support widespread vaccination, for example?

Recommendations

As the main objective of this project is to identify the ethical gaps, barriers and challenges currently present in obtaining informed consent from patients in different, challenging contexts and address the issues with some practical suggestions for future policies, two main deliverables can be extracted from the inputs here analysed. They should be further expanded and taken into consideration when developing new models and forms that aim at providing convincing guidelines for the informed consent process.

The first aspect to take into account is the role of religious keywords. Implementation of some key terms directly refers to some religious traditions. For example, *kosher* or *halal* in vaccines, or reference to *xiaodao* and *dadao* as notions helpful to conceptualize better why we, as single individuals, should behave in a certain way in relation to society. Not only ensuring the "religious approval" from different traditions will increase the trust towards doctors and researchers, but it will also make more evident and immediate in the eyes of the believer terms that will help him filling up required forms and documents with more conviction, speeding up the process of sharing scientific information.

The second point is that international accepted notions and values, such as human duties,[13] should be considered when discussing informed consent, not only human rights. Where possible, use the specific tradition to reinforce the duties towards society as a whole. For example, the principle of the public interest (*maslahat al-ummah*) that sees vaccines as a way to protect *others* in Islam. Or the idea of *dharma* in the Hindu tradition in relation to laws and duties towards society (stressed by many other traditions through different concepts, notions and approaches but still very similar in practice).

These are the final recommendations to increase the effectiveness of multicultural and interreligious perspective:

- Taking into account that not all traditions and religions give the same level of importance to the individual-centred version of autonomy at the base of the informed consent form conceived to be signed by a single individual.
- Implementing some key terms directly referring to some cultural and religious traditions. Considering other key notions such as human duties, not only human rights.
- Fostering participation of trained cross-cultural professionals as members of the ethical research committees to validate cultural and religious concerns during research. Increasing the diversity of the healthcare professionals, improve the opportunity to have individuals capable to filter more directly certain scientific notions into some religious and traditional guidelines.
- Stimulating the composition of cross-cultural research teams, facilitating an understanding of cultural and religious diversity when recruiting and when carrying out research in patients with different cultural backgrounds and religious convictions.
- Capturing the patient religious or cultural background to allow the researcher to introduce appropriate religious and cultural concepts (or terms), when necessary, in the IC form and during the communication process, facilitating the understanding, trust and acceptance of believers towards social value of science and research, improving the acceptance rate of participation in clinical trial.
- Changing the categorization of the patients focusing on a shared common cultural identity. Healthcare professionals should ask questions about other social identities to shift their attention from the patient's ethnicity or religious background helping to reduce racial or cultural biases to improve recruitment of minorities.
- Fostering the religious and community leaders' analysis and possible support or approval of specific scientific biomedical research (i.e. specific therapy or vaccines) so that their support might illuminate believers and increase the trust towards doctors and researchers as well as participation in clinical trials.

Notes

1 The full report can be accessed here: https://i-consentproject.eu/wp-content/uploads/2019/01/D1.4-Ethical-issues-concerning-informed-consent-in-translationalclinical-research-and-vaccination.pdf.
2 UNESCO IBC (2008), 15, https://unesdoc.unesco.org/ark:/48223/pf0000178124.
3 Rachel E. Spector, *Cultural Diversity in Health and Illness* (Upper Saddle River, NJ: Prentice Hall, 2000). Antonella Surbone, "Telling the Truth to Patients with Cancer: What Is the Truth?," *Oncology* 7 (2006): 994–950.
4 Joseph Tham and Marie-Catherine Letendre, "Health Care Decision Making: Cross-Cultural Analysis of the Shift from the Autonomous to the Relational Self," *The New Bioethics* 20, no. 2 (2014): 180–181.
5 Loredana Persampieri, i-CONSENT December Workshop, Rome, Italy (2017). (unpublished).
6 UNESCO Declaration on Bioethics and Human Rights (2005), Art. 12.
7 Italian Committee for Bioethics (2017), 38, http://bioetica.governo.it/media/1391/p128_2017_immigrazione-e-salute_it.pdf.
8 Dan M. Kahan, et al., "Who Fears the HPV Vaccine, Who Doesn't, and Why? An Experimental Study of the Mechanisms of Cultural Cognition," *Law and Human Behavior* 34, no. 6 (2010): 501–516.
9 Simon Dein and Kamaldeep Bhui, "Issues Concerning Informed Consent for Medical Research among Non-Westernized Ethnic Minority Patients in the UK," *Journal of the Royal Society of Medicine* 98, no. 8 (2005): 354–356.
10 General Medical Council, *Consent: Patients and Doctors Making Decisions Together* (2008), www.gmc-uk.org/-/media/documents/gmc-guidance-for-doctors---consent---english_pdf-48903482.pdf.
11 Tami Lynn Thomas, et al., "Parental Human Papillomavirus Vaccine Survey (PHPVS): Nurse-Led Instrument Development and Psychometric Testing for Use in Research and Primary Care Screening," *Journal of Nursing Measurement* 21, no. 1 (2013): 96–109.
12 John D. Grabenstein, "What the World's Religions Teach, Applied to Vaccines and Immune Globulins," *Vaccine* 31, no. 16 (2013): 2011–2023.
13 Fundación Valecia Tercer Milenio, *Declaration of Human Duties and Responsibilities* (1999), http://unesdoc.unesco.org/Ulis/cgi-bin/ulis.pl?catno=188520&gp=&lin=1&ll=f.

2 Informed consent and minors in a multicultural society

Mirko Daniel Garasic and Fabio Macioce

Minors' participation in clinical research trials

According to the World Medical Association's Declaration of Helsinki: "while the primary purpose of medical research is to generate new knowledge, this goal can never take precedence over the rights and interests of individual research subjects."[1] Hence, voluntary and informed consent is a necessary condition. However, if trials need to involve persons unable to consent, the duty to protect them becomes pivotal. A strict interpretation of this duty could leave groups of vulnerable people without significant benefits and knowledge about their condition. Hence, we need to justify the involvement of minors and those unable to consent in clinical trials.

Due to the minors' incomplete physical and psychological development, their vulnerability is a preliminary question on every ethical discussion about paediatric clinical trials. Above all, there is a risk of harm because children cannot protect themselves, and official documents have highlighted this reality. Besides the risk of damage to health, the protection of children's rights and proper acquisition of informed consent could be legal and ethical in a multicultural society such as ours. We will employ a multicultural approach if it does not infringe upon fundamental human rights.

Given the low involvement rates presently, children's participation in clinical trials is considered insufficient.

> The reasons for these deficits are to be found in a lack of interest on the part of the pharmaceutical industry, firstly because of the lower economic potential (smaller markets) and secondly because studies involving children are more complex, time-consuming, and expensive. This is enhanced by the fact that the conditions of trials change depending on the different stages of childhood development and the related risks are therefore more difficult to assess.[2]

DOI: 10.4324/9781003213215-4

In research, it is essential to involve people who cannot consent, including children, so that they can assess benefits for their health, balanced with related risks. For these reasons, various institutional documents have highlighted the importance of informed consent, risk assessment and inclusion criteria in clinical trials on human subjects. We need to handle these issues carefully when dealing with minors because they cannot understand the technical information and freely give consent.[3]

First and foremost, we need to stress the necessity and utmost importance of paediatric clinical trials. Official documents request children involved in scientific research: "Growth and maturation processes, as well as certain specific diseases are unique to children. Specific consequences of medical interventions may be seen in children and may only appear long after exposure."[4] Therefore, from an ethical perspective, their involvement in clinical research need not be viewed as a necessary evil.

> In the past, many new products were not tested in children or adolescents although they were directed at diseases also occurring in childhood. In some cases, this resulted in children or adolescents being exposed to interventions that were either not effective or harmful. In general, this lack of information results in higher risks for children and adolescents from being exposed to interventions where little is known about their specific effects or safety in this population. Therefore, it is imperative to involve children.[5]

Nevertheless, minors' involvement in clinical research is not advised if trials can be carried out on adult subjects: research should be carried out first among less vulnerable subjects.[6] About the order of involvement in research, it is often preferable to experiment on adults before children. Nonetheless, the Council for International Organizations of Medical Sciences (CIOMS) does not establish such a strict requirement because children may face different health issues, and their specific conditions may have been considered. However, older children with greater capacity to consent should be involved before younger children, except for special scientific reasons.[7]

Trials involving minors are essential to test the effects of therapies and interventions or develop observational studies.[8] To offer tailored and better healthcare for children, paediatric clinical trials are necessary to understand their particular physiological characteristics and health needs. CIOMS states that "children and adolescents must be included in health-related research unless a good scientific reason justifies their exclusion."[9] Minors' condition requires a series of specific protections, above all because they cannot consent. However, their exclusion from trials needs to have a sound scientific basis concerning the risks and benefits of their involvement.

In line with this, the Nuffield Council on Bioethics affirms that children's welfare is an essential aspect to consider. However, this welfare should encompass possible scientific contributions that could benefit all children in the future.[10] It does not imply a moral duty for children and parents to consent, but an aspect to determine what is good for children.

What are the risks and benefits for minors?

Clinical research on human subjects has allowed a significant increase in therapeutic and diagnostic opportunities. However, it is structurally uncertain because it is built on a scientific hypothesis that must be confirmed through investigation. Parents and society oversee children's protection, which requires risk and burden minimization and benefit calculation.[11] Hence, researchers must minimize risks and burdens, balancing them with expected benefits for subjects and improvement of knowledge.

Risk assessment is a fundamental aspect of a research protocol. In paediatric clinical trials, it requires strict control:

> Risk assessment includes the evaluation of the risk of the medicinal product tested or the control, the risk of withholding active treatment in some cases, the risk of the disease itself. Potential harms would include invasiveness and intrusiveness of research, the severity as well as seriousness of potential harms, the reversibility of adverse effects and reactions, and their preventability. The accumulation of research projects in the same population (over-studied population) is another potential harm. Multiple clinical trials in an individual should be discouraged.[12]

Significant risks in clinical trials are related to the health of the subjects and data reliability. Health-related risks depend on prior experiences with the intervention/product to be tested and their nature. If the risk is minimal, we can involve children, considering the benefits they may get compared to standard clinical treatment. These benefits can be direct or indirect. The direct benefit is health recovery by treating the patient's condition. The indirect benefit comes from general medical knowledge about the condition of the patient and others who are similarly affected or general knowledge that can benefit society.[13] Having direct benefits is essential to justify therapeutic interventions. It is also important in clinical trials, "In scientific research projects, a potential direct benefit also plays a key role in the ethical evaluation of the trial."[14]

CIOMS adds: "When the social value of the studies with such research interventions and procedures is compelling, and these studies cannot be conducted in adults, a research ethics committee may permit a minor increase above minimal risk."[15]

Usually, "minimal risk" means that the probability and magnitude of harm or discomfort anticipated in the research are not greater in and of themselves than those ordinarily encountered in daily life or during the performance of routine physical or psychological examinations or tests. However, this definition also lends itself to ambiguous interpretations.

In addition to risks, the burden of minors involved in research is more significant than adults. There could be anxieties, pain or interference in children's daily activities, such as separations from parents during the clinical trials, frequent invasive procedures or burdensome side effects. Parents are usually more focused on their children's life and health risks, but we must also consider the harmful effects of different burdens.

Healthy children should not be involved in clinical trials because they cannot provide proper informed consent. Prevention trials or vaccine trials are justified exceptions because, in these cases, they are preventive measures with a good risk/benefit ratio both for individuals and for society. However, they must be carried out following high standards of safety.

Research integrity, ethics review and undue inducement

The exploitation of people unable to consent is unacceptable, and a mandatory review by ethics committees is essential.[16] We need to ensure research integrity by compliance with ethical principles and professional standards.[17]

Research ethics committees have an essential role in reviewing protocols and ensuring the "ethical acceptability" of the research.[18] In paediatric trials, research ethics committees will need to involve children's healthcare specialists to assess the risks and burdens of envisaged procedures adequately. They need to scrutinize both the scientific and ethical aspects with ethical and peer reviews. The ethics committee or competent authorities should not allow the trial to proceed when ethical guidelines are not followed.

Parents may consult their child's physician about participating in a clinical trial. If the physician is the investigator, we need to make sure there is no undue influence and conflict of interests. Concerns about access to regular care should not influence the desire to participate in a clinical trial. If the researcher oversees the caring of minors involved in clinical trials, commitment to investigate cannot override the duty to care. The desire for successful research outcomes cannot compromise the proper treatment of the patient.[19]

Children and family autonomy in a multicultural society

When research involves ethnic minorities, informed consent and autonomy may even be more challenging and complicated. In its Report on Traditional Medicine Systems and their Ethical Implications, UNESCO's International Bioethics Committee addresses the challenge of cultural diversity in healthcare and medicine. It emphasizes that non-Western traditions may have a different approach to life, death, health and illness and so entail a different view regarding the patient, practitioner, patient/practitioner relationship, health services, and risk factors.[20] In other words, it recognizes that Western medicine is grounded on a specific view of the human being and reflects a specific understanding of human life which may be different from that of the patient.

This difference must not be overestimated, of course. For instance, the relationship between health conceptions and ethnic identities is not completely clear. The definition of ethnic minority is problematic,[21] and it may even be more arduous when we look at health-related issues. If we consider characteristics of culture, religion, language and traditions that make ethnic members different from the rest of the population, they also preserve a sense of solidarity of these groups.[22] The relevance of some health traditions and conceptions that preserve ethnic identity is not easy to understand. Health conceptions, more than other issues, transcend the minorities' limits.

When a specific health tradition is relevant for the minority's identity, the balance between recognizing such a tradition and the defence of individual freedom and rights is highly problematic. While this question is of general relevance concerning subgroups, it becomes even more complicated when it relates to health challenges.[23] This is because Western health laws (we may consider both U.S. and E.U.) are rooted in a few principles: patient autonomy, freedom of treatment, informed consent, giving a clear priority to the single individual and his/her rights over the group.[24]

Some barriers may become evident when ethnic subgroups take part in clinical trials.[25] They include language barriers and limits to the comprehensibility of information concerning different linguistic uses, concepts of disease or ways of expressing sensations and attitudes regarding disease and well-being. Second, barriers may come from the individuals' different roles within the community, the group they belong to and the family. Finally, barriers may derive from a limited knowledge of research practices, procedures and ethical and legal constraints.

When we conceptualize the idea of preserving a young patient's "best interest," we tend to have an idealized version of what that patient would do or want us to do, which amounts to preserving; defending or increasing their values, priorities and autonomy. Indeed, there is a tendency to associate individual rights with individual autonomy and a corresponding uneasiness to associate the patient's interest with a non-individualistic version of autonomy. We need to pay attention to how it can create frictions in the healthcare system. We have discussed elsewhere the distinction between relational and individual autonomy.[26] Here, we want to question some of the main legislative tools used in clinical research involving minors based on an individualistic understanding of autonomy.

According to O'Neill,[27] the limits of the moral validity of individual autonomy lie in the implicit acceptance of independence as the most critical value among others to shape human beings. Relational autonomy grants an alternative conceptualization of freedom and self-government in a socially constituted agent who is equally committed to personal preferences, interpersonal relations and mutual dependencies. Accordingly, the exercise of patient autonomy largely depends on the resources available for the individual, institutional facilities and legal instruments.

Among these facilities and instruments, social rights are of primary importance. They provide the subject with goods and resources which make autonomy possible: education, healthcare assistance, welfare and participation of one's cultural and religious life.[28] Moreover, autonomy requires the subject to be inserted in a relational context suitable for the exercise of freedom and characterized by positive relations of recognition. Autonomous choices, recognized by the subject as their own and correspond to their goals, depend on a series of supporting conditions that are normative, institutional and social (or more generically relational).[29] Due to this complex interplay between personal capacities, institutional context and relational resources, autonomy is a concept that has variance in degrees. Conditions that support autonomy can strengthen or weaken it.

For example, in paediatric clinical trials, the subjects do not have full individual autonomy to become involved. This vulnerable group (minors and their families) needs to decide in a context of uncertainty. Hence, minors need appropriate support from adults, first from parents, but also researchers and society. As a result, specific protections are required. CIOMS states that before starting a paediatric clinical trial, researchers and ethics committees should safeguard that

> 1) a parent or a legally authorized representative of the child or adolescent has given permission; and 2) the agreement (assent) of the child or adolescent has been obtained in keeping with the child's or adolescent's capacity, after having been provided with adequate information about the research tailored to the child's or adolescent's level of maturity.[30]

Most official documents accept vulnerability as a significant concern. Vulnerability requires protection, but such protection can restrict the right to participate in decision-making and obtain benefits from clinical trials. There is a tension between the need to avoid harm and the right to be informed and make choices. The Nuffield Council on Bioethics challenges the correlation between vulnerability and childhood. It invites researchers to work in partnership with children and parents and not to only protect children "from" research.[31] It means that minors must be encouraged to participate and make decisions. Their autonomy and integrity must be respected by giving importance to their views, listening to them and allowing their participation in decision-making. Once again, not everyone would necessarily agree on what their "autonomy" comprises and how to respect it genuinely. Crucial to this assessment are the roles of parents, which we will now investigate.

The roles of parents

Parental involvements are vital, from both legal and ethical points of view. They not only have the right to decide or duty to protect, but also assist and support their children's evolving autonomy. Parents should evaluate their "children's best interests," a complex concept decided on a case-by-case basis, considering their needs and rights. In the field of research involving minors, the notion of "avoidance of harm" may be more objective than that of "best interest." The "best interest" approach generally weighs each case's potential benefits and burdens. However, in clinical research, it is considered too generic, lending itself to ambiguous interpretations.

Since the participant's interest is not the only focus of clinical trials, the Nuffield Council on Bioethics sustains that parental consent to research "should be based on their confidence that participation in the proposed research is compatible with their child's immediate and longer-term interests."[32] Thus, the minors' "best interest," which is fundamental in clinical practice, does not become the only consideration in decision-making, overriding other ethical values.

Nevertheless, parents need decision-making support. In difficult situations, clinical trials involve burdens or risks. When parents need to deal with their children's illness which can be severe, the distress could compromise their judgement capacity. In chronic illnesses, children may have greater experience and capacity to understand the risks, burdens and benefits of a clinical trial than their parents.

Suppose that it is impossible to obtain parental permission in an emergency. In that case, the ethical review board can grant approval and then inform and involve parents as soon as possible. If the children can understand and decide in these circumstances, their decision should be respected.[33]

According to the U.S. Institute of Medicine, ethical review committees can waive parental permission in clinical trials of adolescents when 1) the research is essential to the health and well-being of adolescents and cannot reasonably or practically be carried out without the waiver; 2) the research involves treatments that State laws permit adolescents to receive without parental permission; 3) when the investigator has presented evidence that the adolescents are capable of understanding the research and their rights as research participants and 4) the research protocol includes appropriate safeguards to protect the adolescent's interests consistent with the risks of the trial.[34]

Parents cannot ask their children to become involved in clinical research without sound scientific evidence adequately evaluated by researchers and ethics committees. Even here, some axioms are not as simple as they might first appear. We mention only one example. The standard of bodily integrity, required by the Nuffield Council on Bioethics, is challenged by a substantial portion of the world with the practice of male circumcision. We cannot dwell on this very delicate matter here.[35] Suffice it to say that this standard is not defended as vigorously or convincingly when applied in different contexts.

Children and mature minors: different age, different issues

As children mature in age, their capacity to understand takes on greater validity, and individual autonomy becomes important. To be a "minor" is a legal status, as the law fixes the age of adulthood conventionally. Nonetheless, to be a child or a young person is foremost an existential condition. The minors' continuous development becomes an ethical issue since there are significant differences between infants, children and youth. "What is more difficult and especially deserves 'ethical weighing' is research on children as children continually develop their ability to give consent as they grow older."[36]

Some groups have proposed an age-based classification. ICH distinguishes between newborns (0–27 days), infants and toddlers (28 days–23 months), children (2–11 years) and adolescents (12–18 years). In the same document, ICH states that "any classification of the paediatric population into age categories is to some extent arbitrary," but still useful for study design.[37] EMA makes no distinction between minors and children, using these terms synonymously.[38] Nevertheless, they consider consent and its value according to age groups and the subjects' maturity. It is impossible to obtain valid assent from children between birth and three years of age. There is no specific indication for 3–6-years-old. For children of school age (from 6 years of age onwards), providing information and obtaining assent are recommended. From the age of 9, children are considered capable of understanding information. Adolescents are more independent and need respect and not only protection of their autonomy. "Assent from an adolescent who is a minor should be sought, and, where possible respected."[39] Researchers must, however, evaluate if adolescents have understood the information provided.

If clinical research implies minimal risks and burden for minors, the Austrian Bioethics Commission requires parental permission only for children under 14.

> For minors aged 14 or older (mature minors), the Bioethics Commission does not envisage such a requirement as mature minors are allowed to act independently also in the case of other comparable medical measures. Group benefit research shall be enabled for this group of persons beyond the scope of the special laws.[40]

Without fixing a rigid age threshold, the Nuffield Council on Bioethics distinguishes three different situations when dealing with the broad concept of "childhood":[41]

> *Case One:* children who cannot give an opinion if they should take part in the research. They could be babies and very young children, or children who are temporarily unable to opine because they are unwell or unconscious.
> *Case Two:* children who can form views and express wishes but cannot yet make independent decisions about research involvement.
> *Case Three:* children and young people who potentially have the intellectual capacity and maturity to make decisions about participation in research but are considered minors in their local legal system.

Case One includes all children at the beginning of life. For children in *Case Three*, their assent is as good as informed consent.

> We recommend that, where children and young people have sufficient maturity and understanding but are not yet treated as fully 'adult' by the law of their country, professionals should, wherever possible, seek consent from both the children or young people concerned, and from their parents.[42]

According to CIOMS:

> As adolescents near the age of majority, their agreement to participate in research may be ethically (though not legally) equivalent to consent. In this situation, parental consent is ethically best considered as

'co-consent' but legally, the adolescent's agreement remains assent. If child or adolescent participants reach the legal age of majority according to applicable law and become capable of independent informed consent during the research, their written informed consent to continued participation must be sought and their decision respected.[43]

The International Bioethics Committee of UNESCO states that the "criteria for the capacity to consent have included the ability to understand the issues involved in the decisions at stake, the ability to evaluate these rationally, a reasonable outcome of the decision and evidence of a decision being made."[44]

Some jurisdictions recognize the status of "emancipated" minors who are not living with their parents and eventually have their own families. Emancipated minors can be married or parents themselves, so they can request the involvement of adults who are not their parents. "If an adolescent aged 16 to 18 is no longer a minor as defined in national law, or is an 'emancipated minor,' then written informed consent is required from these individuals as for any adult capable of giving consent. Under these conditions, informed consent is no longer required from the parents/legal representative, although an adolescent is still vulnerable and may require additional discussions and explanations."[45]

In long-term clinical trials, investigators should periodically check the minors' maturity and their capacity to consent. They should seek their assent or informed consent when appropriate or once the research subjects have reached the legal age.[46]

The example of emancipated minors highlights yet another evolution of individual/relational autonomy that requires greater attention. It is peculiar that the decisive factor in "elevating" emancipated minors to fully competent adults is when they have formed their own families. In other words, we give as much importance to the role of *relationships* (becoming accountable and responsible adults through parenthood) as the personal capacity to process information. On balance, we have consigned relational autonomy a more significant role than we might have realized.

Conclusion

Through documents of eminent health and bioethical organizations in the world, we have seen how the current conceptualization of autonomy is biased towards individualism. In the light of the increasingly multicultural societies we live in, these assumptions should not go unchallenged. We have seen some legal shortcomings of informed consent in clinical research, especially in minors. We call for further analysis and research on this topic that has made progress but still requires improvements.

Notes

1. World Medical Association, *Declaration of Helsinki (as Amended)* (2013), art. 8, www.wma.net/policies-post/wma-declaration-of-helsinki-ethical-principles-for-medical-research-involving-human-subjects/.
2. Austrian Bioethics Commission, *Research on Persons without the Capacity to Consent-with Special Consideration of the Concept of Risk* (2013), 34, www.oeaw.ac.at/resources/Record/990002754000504498.
3. European Medicines Agency (EMA), *Guideline for Good Clinical Practice* (2016), www.ema.europa.eu/en/ich-e6-r2-good-clinical-practice.
4. European Medicines Agency, *Ethical Considerations for Clinical Trials on Medicinal Products Conducted with Paediatric Population* (2008), 4, https://ec.europa.eu/health//sites/health/files/files/eudralex/vol-10/ethical_considerations_en.pdf.
5. Council for International Organizations of Medical Sciences (CIOMS), *International Ethical Guidelines for Health-Related Research Involving Humans*, Commentary on Guideline, (2016), 17, https://cioms.ch/publications/product/international-ethical-guidelines-for-health-related-research-involving-humans/.
6. EMA (2008), 5.
7. CIOMS (2016).
8. Austrian Bioethics Commission (2013), 36.
9. CIOMS (2016).
10. Nuffield Council on Bioethics, *Children and Clinical Research: Ethical Issues* (2015), para 4.28, www.nuffieldbioethics.org/publications/children-and-clinical-research
11. International Conference on Harmonisation of Technical Requirements for Registration of Pharmaceuticals for Human Use-ICH, *E 11: Clinical Investigation of Medicinal Products in the Paediatric Population* (2000), www.ema.europa.eu/en/documents/scientific-guideline/international-conference-harmonisation-technical-requirements-registration-pharmaceuticals-human-use_en-1.pdf; World Health Organization (WHO), *Standards and Operational Guidance for Ethics Review of Health-Related Research with Human Participants* (2011), www.who.int/ethics/publications/9789241502948/en/; European Commission, *Report from the Commission to the European Parliament and the Council: Better Medicines for Children:—From Concept to Reality* (2013), https://ec.europa.eu/health/sites/health/files/files/paediatrics/2013_com443/paediatric_report-com%282013%29443_en.pdf; CIOMS (2016).
12. EMA (2008), 17.
13. French National Consultative Ethics Committee for Health and Life Sciences, *Ethical Issues Raised by Collections of Biological Material and Associated Information Data: "Biobanks," "Libraries,"* (2003), 3–5, www.ccne-ethique.fr/sites/default/files/publications/avis077en.pdf.
14. Austrian Bioethics Commission (2013), 39.
15. CIOMS (2016).
16. Council of Europe, Committee on Bioethics-DH-BIO, *Guide for Research Ethics Committee Members* (2012), 40, www.coe.int/en/web/bioethics/guide-for-research-ethics-committees-members.
17. European Group on Ethics in Science and New Technologies, *Statement on the Formulation of a Code of Conduct for Research Integrity for Projects Funded by the European Commission* (2015), https://ec.europa.eu/info/sites/default/files/research_and_innovation/ege/research_integrity_ege_statement.pdf.
18. WHO (2011), 12.

19 Nuffield Council on Bioethics (2015), xxxiii.
20 UNESCO (IBC), *Report of the IBC on Traditional Medicine Systems and Their Ethical Implications* (2013), 12, https://unesdoc.unesco.org/ark:/48223/pf0000217457_eng.
21 Jennifer Jackson-Preece, "Beyond the (Non) Definition of Minority," *European Centre for Minority Issues (ECMI) Brief* (2014), 30, www.ecmi.de/publications/issue-briefs/beyond-the-non-definition-of-minority.
22 Francesco Capotorti, *Study of the Rights of the Persons Belonging to Ethnic, Religious and Linguistic Minorities* (New York: UN, E/CN.4/Sub.2/384/Rev.1, 1979), https://digitallibrary.un.org/record/10387.
23 Leslie Green, "Internal Minorities and Their Rights," in *Group Rights*, ed. Judith Baker (Toronto, ON: University of Toronto Press, 1994), 71; Avigail Eisenberg, *Reasons of Identity: A Normative Guide to the Political and Legal Assessment of Identity Claims* (New York: Oxford University Press, 2009); Avigail Eisenberg and Jeff Spinner-Halev, "Introduction," in *Minorities within Minorities: Equality, Rights and Diversity*, ed. Avigail Eisenberg and Jeff Spinner-Halev (Cambridge: Cambridge University Press, 2005), 1–15.
24 Raanan Gillon, "Ethics Needs Principles:—Four Can Encompass the Rest:—And Respect for Autonomy Should Be 'First among Equals'," *Journal of Medical Ethics* 29, no. 5 (2003): 307–312.
25 Simon Dein and Kamaldeep Bhui, "Issues Concerning Informed Consent for Medical Research among Non-Westernized Ethnic Minority Patients in the UK," *Journal of the Royal Society of Medicine* 98, no. 8 (2005): 354–356.
26 Mirko Daniel Garasic, *Guantanamo and Other Cases of Enforced Medical Treatment:—A Biopolitical Analysis* (New York: Springer, 2015); Fabio Macioce, "Between Autonomy and Vulnerability: Rethinking Informed Consent in a Relational Perspective," *Notizie di POLITEIA* 35, no. 134 (2019): 111–128.
27 Onora O'Neill, *Autonomy and Trust in Bioethics* (Cambridge: Cambridge University Press, 2002).
28 Robert Young, *Autonomy: Beyond Negative and Positive Liberty* (New York: St. Martin's Press, 1986); Joseph Raz, *The Morality of Freedom* (Oxford: Clarendon Press, 1986); Marina Oshana, "Personal Autonomy and Society," *The Journal of Social Philosophy* 29 (1998): 81–102; Amartya Sen, *Development as Freedom* (New York: Knopf. A., 1999).
29 Joel Anderson, "Disputing Autonomy: Second-Order Desires and the Dynamics of Ascribing Autonomy," *Sats:—Nordic Journal of Philosophy* 9, no. 1 (2008): 7–26.
30 CIOMS (2016).
31 Nuffield Council on Bioethics (2015), para 4.5.
32 *Ibid.*, para 4.33.
33 *Ibid.*, para 6.35.
34 Institute of Medicine of the U.S. National Academy of Sciences, *Ethical Conduct of Clinical Research Involving Children* (Washington, DC: The National Academies Press, 2004), 201. https://doi.org/10.17226/10958.
35 For further information on this, see Mirko Daniel Garasic, "In Defence of Male Circumcision," *Monash Bioethics Review* 31, no. 1 (2013): 60–69.
36 Austrian Bioethics Commission (2013), 44.
37 ICH (2000), 7.
38 EMA (2008), 7.
39 *Ibid.*, 12.

40 Austrian Bioethics Commission (2013), 46.
41 Nuffield Council on Bioethics (2015), para 4.5.
42 *Ibid.*, recommendation 13.
43 CIOMS (2016).
44 UNESCO (IBC), *Report of the IBC on Consent*, no. 79 (2008), https://ethics.iarc.fr/Documents/IBC_consent.pdf.
45 EMA (2008), 10.
46 *Ibid.*; International Conference on Harmonisation of Technical Requirements for Registration of Pharmaceuticals for Human Use (ICH), *Addendum to E 11: Clinical Investigation of Medicinal Products in the Paediatric Population* (2016), 5, www.ema.europa.eu/en/ich-e11r1-step-5-guideline-clinical-investigation-medicinal-products-pediatric-population; Italian Committee for Bioethics, *Clinical Trials in Adult or Minor Patients Who Are Unable to Give Informed Consent in Emergencies* (2012), http://bioetica.governo.it/en/opinions/opinions-responses/clinical-trials-in-adult-or-minor-patients-who-are-unable-to-give-informed-consent-in-emergency-situations/; Italian Committee for Bioethics, *Paediatric Biobanks* (2014), 11, http://bioetica.governo.it/en/opinions/opinions-responses/pediatric-biobanks/.

3 Community engagement in the informed consent process in global clinical research
International recommendations and guidelines

Margherita Daverio

Challenges to informed consent in global clinical research and the need for community involvement

Informed consent is not only a written form or a bureaucratic procedure but also, above all, an essential communication process between the participant and the researcher in clinical research. In many cases, obtaining informed consent may be difficult with people from diverse cultural backgrounds. It could happen in the context of global clinical research, particularly in the case of international multicentre studies where researchers and the potential participants belong to different cultural contexts.[1]

To overcome communication barriers and avoid misconceptions and misunderstandings, interaction in a multicultural setting cannot overlook cultural diversity, as it contributes to shaping subjective identities. Thus, cultural diversity affects the way people process and understand information.

Cultural differences between researchers and potential participants in clinical trials could result in communication barriers which are likely to hinder awareness and pose challenges to the informed consent process.[2] In 2015, the World Health Organization (WHO) emphasized that "a challenge in global health ethics concerns international research, especially where investigators from wealthy countries conduct research in impoverished settings where participants are especially vulnerable or where language and cultural barriers make informed consent difficult."[3] In addition, in cross-cultural communication—as in the case of specific international multicentre clinical trials in the context of global health-related research—special care is generally recommended in collecting informed consent to avoid the risk of possible poor communication due to language differences.[4] Moreover, sound comprehension of information becomes complex when those who intervene do not use the same references in approaching health problems. For example, the scientific approach of a research team is different from a

DOI: 10.4324/9781003213215-5

mystical, supernatural approach to health which could be found in some communities.[5]

We can identify as follows three major areas of barriers in cross-cultural communication:

a) language barriers;[6] in some communities, there could not even be the word to express some scientific concepts related to research, for example, for the term "randomization";[7] a study from the United Kingdom about the inclusion of non-English-speaking patients in the research-reported language barriers and the unavailability of translators for different reasons;[8]
b) lack of awareness about trials and shallow understanding of the concept of research, which may be confused with the direct health services provision; in general, difficulties in understanding research process;[9]
c) lack of trust in researchers and low health literacy regarding immunization; concern about adverse events and fears about exploitation (especially in the case of healthy volunteers, as it is in the case of experimental vaccines).[10]

A scientific paper highlighted several issues in the considered area (Kenya and sub-Saharan Africa) that undermined informed consent processes.[11] These include limited exposure to research concepts and procedures, a lack of local terms for critical elements of research, rumours about research activities and their purposes, such as taking blood samples from healthy children. In addition, there could be difficulties for potential participants in understanding large volumes of research-related information, especially when children are sick and consenting processes are deemed to be delaying initiation of treatment. Finally, perceptions that research procedures are part of standard care (therapeutic misconceptions) or vice versa and lack of in-depth understanding of research or research ethics among those responsible for explaining research activities can hinder proper communication in the informed consent process. To respond to these challenges, researchers implemented informed consent forms prepared directly in the local language with the help of community members.[12]

Therefore, community engagement in research has gained consideration as an approach "helping ensure that community concerns are taken into account and to informing ethical decision-making when research is conducted in context of vulnerability."[13] During the whole informed consent process, community collaboration is essential to prevent researchers who are not local to a community from making assumptions about how to research and giving advice for conducting the process for seeking consent in a culturally tailored way.[14] Relationships between communities and researchers can take different forms, ranging from community consultation in specific stages of the research to community representation during the whole research process and even to a long-term and more complex partnership. Different types of community involvement could be appropriate in different situations; for example, informal consultations could be enough for some studies, but in others, especially when vulnerable populations are involved, there could be a need for a formal consultation or partnership.[15] In this perspective, community engagement becomes an essential part of research to meet each community's needs and priorities and overcome cultural challenges and communication barriers.

Ethical goals of community engagement in collaborative research

Community engagement is a recognized ethical requirement in health-related research.[16] A community consists not only of people living in the geographic area where research is to be carried out, but it also comprises "different sectors of society that have a stake in the proposed research, as well as sub-populations from which research participants will be recruited."[17] Engagement has ethical implications—ethics does not stop when community engagement takes place: "Engagement is about 'exchange.' It is not about providing information or disseminating ideas or results. Communities can also drive the engagement process, holding scientists and science accountable for their ethics. Suppose a good relationship is already established between scientists and communities. In that case, it is possible to do a short piece of research that also engages the community as a matter of principle."[18] In addition, community engagement is a form of patient and public involvement (PPI). PPI in research can potentially help researchers make sure that their research design is relevant that is participant friendly and ethically sound.[19] Community engagement could then be described as a double-way process, a mutual aid between the community and the research team and vice versa.[20]

To overcome the most frequent challenges to the informed consent process in the context of global health-related research, community engagement practices can promote a significant involvement of local people. Notably, community members should be invited to develop the informed consent process and documents to ensure that they are understandable and appropriate for potential participants. To face language barriers, the involvement of community members in the preparation of informed consent materials can help. For example, they can suggest how to explain to potential participants concepts that could be difficult to understand, such as "placebo," "randomization" and advising on how to provide information in a culturally sensitive way.[21] To prevent from possible cultural barriers, potential cultural sensitivities should be explored in advance of biomedical research with the help of local communities. The contribution of potential local participants and local researchers can prevent violating customary practices.[22] This contribution often can come through the contribution of the local trusted "spokesperson," persons who not only can translate but also help understand cultural values and perceptions; one of these persons could be a contact person between the community and the research team.

Three main arguments supporting community engagement could be identified.[23] They reflect the main ethical goals of community engagement:

1. Protecting communities. Informing and consulting members of the broader community on the ongoing research is seen as additional protection for the ethical conduct of the research besides that provided by ethics committee approvals and informed;[24]
2. Improving research quality. Community involvement has the potential to increase study efficiency in several steps: the better informed a community is about a study, the easier it will be to improve the recruitment process; research could benefit from a paradigm shift in which community involvement is seen as a way to achieve higher research quality;[25]
3. Building trust. Involving the community in the research is one way to build mutual trust with the population and show respect to all affected by the research, beyond the study participants. Building trust involves the commitment to the well-being of communities and the protection of their interests.[26]

Collaborative research views all stakeholders as equals, and even if the needs and priorities of the community and the researchers are not the same, they should be reciprocal. Increasingly, "international collaborative research is being asked to consider the local interests of resource-constrained partners and the responsibility of collaborations to safeguard against the potential for structural exploitation when operating in resource-constrained settings."[27] Community engagement can set the basis for good collaborative research, which international recommendations and guidelines require, mainly through protecting communities, providing benefits for the community, research quality and building trust and equitable partnership among stakeholders.[28]

Towards a meaningful participatory process. International recommendations and guidelines on community engagement

Community engagement is central to any public health intervention. In 2017, the WHO emphasized its definition of community engagement as "a process of developing relationships that enable stakeholders to work together to address health-related issues and promote well-being to achieve positive health impact and outcomes."[29]

In global clinical research, research can take place also in developing countries. Regarding this specific case, in 2003, the European Group on Ethics in Science and New Technologies (EGE) reminded that "the legitimacy of the objectives of research is related to the analysis of its relevance regarding health priorities of the partners, the risk/benefits balance for individuals and the communities, and the potential impact on healthcare of the host country."[30] To reach this ethical goal, researchers have an additional responsibility towards the community where the clinical trial takes place and should seek agreement as appropriate from people representative of or invested with certain authority in the community. Community engagement is a crucial means to tailor research and particularly informed consent process to the community needs and values. "The application of general ethical standards of clinical trials to the different cultural context, in particular to developing countries, needs in fact an activity of interpretation and specification: this process might be helped by a community consultation to acquire better knowledge of local culture and involving community representatives in the elaboration of research projects."[31]

The Council for International Organizations of Medical Sciences (CIOMS) guidelines in the revised 2016 version include a brand-new guideline devoted explicitly to community engagement. To this aim, Guideline 7 recommends the inclusion of communities in global collaborative research through a "meaningful participatory process, that involves them in an early and sustained manner in the design, development, implementation, design of the informed consent process and monitoring of the research, and in the dissemination of its results."[32]

First, proactive and sustained engagement of communities from which individuals are invited to participate shows respect towards the communities and their traditions and norms.[33] Second, besides successful conduct of research, community engagement is a means of ensuring the relevance of proposed research to the affected community and ensures the ethical and social value and outcome of the proposed research. Third, community engagement is a double-way ongoing process, which promotes reciprocal trust and confidence between researchers and community members. "Active engagement with community members is a mutually educative process, which both enables researchers to learn about communities' cultures and understanding of research-related concepts and contributes to research literacy by educating the community about key concepts critical for understanding the purpose and procedures of the research."[34]

Community engagement implies mutual and reciprocal relationships between the research team and community members. In addition, CIOMS guideline 7 reminds that engaging the community strengthens local ownership of the research and builds confidence in the ability of leaders to negotiate various aspects of the research (recruitment strategies, care for the health needs of study participants, site selection, data collection and sharing and so on).

Engagement is recommended, "at the earliest opportunity." Engaging at the earliest stage promotes smooth study functioning. It contributes to the community's capacity to understand the research process—and by design, as research protocol to be submitted to the research ethics committee should include a detailed description of the plan for community engagement. Although strategies could be different, community engagement should have an established forum for communication between researchers and community members.

According to CIOMS Guideline 8, *Collaborative partnership and capacity building for research and research review*, local capacity building is identified as an ethical aspect. The collaborative partnership helps ensure the social value of research by engaging the communities, thereby focusing on aspects the community considers valuable. The act of entering a partnership in collaborative research has accompanying ethical responsibilities. This marks the need for collaborative research partnerships to contribute to sustainable capacity-building activities that bring structured changes to local skills, knowledge and systems.[35]

Community's permission under no circumstance can substitute individual informed consent.[36] Community consent cannot substitute individual informed consent according to international ethical requirements.[37] On the issue of community consent, it has been emphasized that recognizing the potential for community protection offered by deliberately reflexive ethical review boards, including community consultations, would avoid the problematic notion of "community consent," which on the other side would imply that "communities" can consent to ethical, legally valid and socially meaningful research.[38] As an effective strategy, "both forms of protections—individual informed consent and ethical review of research protocols—should work together in promoting, strengthening, and reinforcing the protection of communities and their individual members involved in biomedical research."[39]

Leading strategies for community involvement in global clinical research

As considered in the previous paragraph, community engagement is an ongoing and continuing process. Specific strategies and approaches should be tailored to the community context.[40]

In this perspective, choosing the most appropriate form of engagement is a delicate commitment. The best methods of engagement are those which are chosen by the community.[41] A general principle is that to achieve successful collaboration with a community, all parties involved need to strive to understand the point of view of "insiders" of the community. In addition to ample information about community engagement, best practices and case studies, the report called "Principles of community engagement" provides nine community engagement principles, which help identify community engagement strategies.[42] Among these principles are researchers should be clear with the community about purposes and goals of engagement; researchers should know as much as possible the local culture they will be going to interact with; direct interaction with members of the community should be promoted; research teams should foster partnerships and collaborative research; researchers should have and show respect for cultural values and belief and the community self-determination; capacity building should be implemented; flexibility should be promoted to meet the community changing needs and research teams should be available to long-term commitment in building trust.

An active community engagement is, therefore, recommended, and strategies and practical advice could be identified as follows:[43]

a) the inclusion of members of the community involved in the clinical trial in the Institutional Review Board, to include community views and perspectives in the ethical review of the study;[44]
b) to build long-term, mutually beneficial relationships between the community and the research team, to be applied before, during and after research studies with different strategies according to different phases of the research study, for example: engaging in full and frank discussions about the potential benefits and harms that the participants and the community might encounter; ensuring the alignment of the research to local needs; paying the due attention to the impact of the study and the study team upon the participants, their families, the local community and the environment; taking the time to ensure that the implications of the study have been fully understood by participants and the community;[45]
c) the consultation with community members,[46] in particular on how to work with the community, for example, providing a forum for discussing and addressing issues arising from participants and community representatives;[47] an ongoing "dialogue" between the researchers and the community about the proposed study and its potential implications, or a more structured consultation that would document the concerns of a community or a socially identifiable group;

d) periodical meetings with local health teams to inform them of potential studies, including meeting in the local languages with the key leaders in the community, including the village head, the religious leaders; community feedback meetings at the end of the trials also proved helpful in informing participants that studies had ended and for sharing study results;[48] collaborative efforts revealed insights about how to convey information about clinical trial participation;

e) In disease outbreaks, community engagement should be reached through social media,[49] particularly as far as preparedness and risk communication is concerned.[50]

To reach community engagement ethical goals, researchers need to be specifically trained.[51]

Could community engagement be a step more towards a relational view of autonomy?

Community engagement in the informed consent process in global clinical research recognizes and considers the value of relational and cultural dimensions of everyone. Community engagement practices respect these dimensions and drive their contributions into the decision-making process, fostering the exercise of autonomy without undermining it.

We suggest that community engagement practices and the involvement of community members in the informed consent process could be thought of as a way of moving towards a relational view of autonomy. This view can be achieved considering the need for community involvement in the research process and decision-making. Accordingly, they consider the cultural and relational dimensions of everyone as described in the previous paragraphs—never overcoming personal autonomy, always protecting and safeguarding individual and free decision-making. This is because the challenge of respecting the autonomy of persons is not to avoid relational dimensions but to include meaningful forms of relationship in the decision-making process.[52]

A growing number of bioethicists and social scientists invoke a "relational turn" in bioethics that moves beyond individualistic towards more relational perspectives.[53] They are sketching a reconfiguration of the principle of autonomy. A relational view of autonomy includes the autonomy of the individual and the reference to the dialogue with the researcher/physician and wife/husband/relatives and members of the community.[54] This approach can provide solutions to ethical and practical problems in clinical practice and research.

A "relational turn" of autonomy should not be confused with collectivism or authoritarian and paternalistic versions of communitarianism.[55] In clinical research and the informed consent process, individual informed consent should not be overwhelmed by community consent, as stated in international recommendations and above-recalled guidelines. However, concerning the autonomy principle, clear emphasis should be devoted to the situated and communal aspects of relational life and interdependence. A person's interests are connected to other people and groups. They could, thus, be read as a call for a degree of relational autonomy. "Not independence, but interdependence, is at the heart of relational notions of autonomy: social surroundings and relationships enable us to flourish and develop a robust capacity for self-determination and identity formation. Relational autonomy can be viewed as a conception of autonomy that places the individual in a socially embedded network of others. Relationships (with family, community, and society), responsibility, care and interdependence are key attributes of relational autonomy: people develop their sense of self and form capacities and life plans through the relationships they forge on a daily and long-term basis. Therefore, relational autonomy asserts that social surroundings and relationships are crucial for developing autonomy and encourages us to act in ways guided by an ethic of trust and care."[56]

In addition, relational autonomy can provide a broader moral framework for the informed consent process, as the individual is, indeed, autonomous, but at the same time, community-oriented and not self-sufficient and independent of others. According to relational autonomy, informed consent can be a process and a non-static concept. In the case of community engagement practices, the process of consultation gives substantive weight to the considerations of relationships, patients as relational beings who are socially embedded.[57] Therefore, a relational concept of autonomy is a precious concept to appeal to in biomedical research and clinical practice to protect rights and dignity.

In this perspective, community engagement intended as a "meaningful participatory process," involving communities, considering relational dimensions, respecting cultural values and always safeguarding personal autonomy could be inserted in the ethical framework of a relational view of autonomy. This view could be deepened, indeed, more than in the space of this chapter.

Notes

1 Henk Ten Have and Bert Gordijn (eds.), *Handbook of Global Bioethics* (Cham, Switzerland: Springer, 2013), 154.
2 i-CONSENT Project, *Ethical and Legal Review of Gender and Age-Related Issues Associated with the Acquisition of Informed Consent*, i-CONSENT Project (2017), https://i-consentproject.eu/wp-content/uploads/2019/02/D1.3_EthicalLegal_20171030_FINAL.pdf; Doris Schroeder, et al., *Ethics Dumping Case Studies*

from North-South Research Collaborations (New York: Springer, 2018), 99–106; i-CONSENT Project, *New Strategies for Increasing Participation of Patients Coming from Different Cultural and Religious Backgrounds* (2019), www.lumsa.it/sites/default/files/link/T2.6%20LUMSA%20summary%20of%20findings_April%2026%202019_final.pdf.

3. World Health Organization, *Global Health Ethics: Key Issues* (2015), https://apps.who.int/iris/bitstream/handle/10665/164576/9789240694033_eng.pdf;jsessionid=77B9CE5DDD86423B93D0BF4868F76E82?sequence=1.

4. UNESCO International Bioethics Committee, *Report of the IBC on Consent* (2008), https://unesdoc.unesco.org/ark:/48223/pf0000178124; The Council of Europe, *Guide for Research Ethics Committee Members, Steering Committee on Bioethics* (2012), www.coe.int/t/dg3/healthbioethic/activities/02_biomedical_research_en/Guide/Guide_EN.pdf; Council for International Organizations of Medical Sciences (CIOMS), *International Ethical Guidelines for Health-Related Research Involving Humans*, Geneva (2016), https://cioms.ch/wp-content/uploads/2017/01/WEB-CIOMS-EthicalGuidelines.pdf, accessed May 17, 2021.

5. UNESCO International Bioethics Committee, *Report of the IBC on Consent*, 106.

6. Schroeder, et al., *Ethics Dumping Case Studies from North-South Research Collaborations*, 99–106; Louise Condon, et al., "Engaging Gypsy, Roma, and Traveller Communities in Research: Maximizing Opportunities and Overcoming Challenges," *Qualitative Health Research* 29, no. 9 (2019): 1324–1333, https://doi.org/10.1177/1049732318813558; Laura Palazzani, *Innovation in Scientific Research and Emerging Technologies: A Challenge to Ethics and Law* (Cham, Switzerland: Springer Nature and G. Giappichelli Editore, 2019).

7. George Okello, et al., "Challenges for Consent and Community Engagement in the Conduct of Cluster Randomized Trial among School Children in Low Income Settings: Experiences from Kenya," *Trials* 14, no. 1 (2013): 142. https://doi.org/10.1186/1745-6215-14-142.

8. Rachel Bernier, et al., "Inclusion of Non-English-Speaking Patients in Research: A Single Institution Experience," *Pediatric Anesthesia* 28, no. 5 (2018): 415–420. https://doi.org/10.1111/pan.13363.

9. Teo Quay, et al., "Barriers and Facilitators to Recruitment of South Asians to Health Research: a Scoping Review," *BMJ Open* 7, no. 5 (2017). https://doi.org/10.1136/bmjopen-2016-014889; Rossybelle P. Amorrortu, et al., "Recruitment of Racial and Ethnic Minorities to Clinical Trials Conducted within Specialty Clinics: An Intervention Mapping approach," *Trials* 19, no. 1 (2018): 1–10. https://doi.org/10.1186/s13063-018-2507-9.

10. Amorrortu, et al., "Recruitment of Racial and Ethnic Minorities"; Joyce L. Browne, et al., "The Willingness to Participate in Biomedical Research Involving Human Beings in Low- and Middle-Income Countries: A Systematic Review," *Tropical Medicine & International Health* 24, no. 3 (2019): 264–279. https://doi.org/10.1111/tmi.13195; Sarah Gehlert and Jessica Mozersky, "Seeing Beyond the Margins: Challenges to Informed Inclusion of Vulnerable Populations in Research," *Journal of Law, Medicine & Ethics* 46, no. 1 (2018): 30–43. https://doi.org/10.1177/1073110518766006; Bernadette Boden-Albala, et al., "Examining Barriers and Practices to Recruitment and Retention in Stroke Clinical Trials," *Stroke* 46, no. 8 (2015): 2232–2237. https://doi.org/10.1161/strokeaha.114.008564.

11. Mwanamvua Boga, et al., "Strengthening the Informed Consent Process in International Health Research through Community Engagement: The KEMRI-Wellcome Trust Research Programme Experience," *PLoS Medicine* 8, no. 9 (2011). https://doi.org/10.1371/journal.pmed.1001089.

12 Boga, et al., "Strengthening the Informed Consent Process."
13 Kathleen M. MacQueen, et al., "Evaluating Community Engagement in Global Health Research: The Need for Metrics," *B.M.C. Medical Ethics*, 16, no. 44 (2015): 1–10.
14 Emily F. Fitzpatrick, et al., "Seeking Consent for Research with Indigenous Communities: A Systematic Review," *BMC Medical Ethics* 17, no. 1 (2016). https://doi.org/10.1186/s12910-016-0139-8.
15 Federica Fregonese, "Community Involvement in Biomedical Research Conducted in the Global Health Context: What Can Be Done to Make It Really Matter?," *BMC Medical Ethics* 19, no. S1 (2018). https://doi.org/10.1186/s12910-018-0283-4.
16 CIOMS, *International Ethical Guidelines*; European Group on Ethics in Science and New Technologies, *Ethical Aspects of Clinical Research in Developing Countries: Opinion* (2003), n. 17, https://publications.europa.eu/en/publication-detail/-/publication/6339dcbf-c156-4e7f-9e43-9928acf82118/language-en/format-PDF/source-77404483.
17 CIOMS, *International Ethical Guidelines*, Commentary on Guideline 7.
18 Wellcome Trust, *Community Engagement:—Under the Microscope: Report of a Workshop in Thailand* (June 12–15, 2011), https://wellcome.ac.uk/sites/default/files/wtvm054326_0.pdf.
19 Heather J. Bagley, Hannah Short, Nicola L. Harman, Helen R. Hickey, Carrol L. Gamble, Kerry Woolfall, Bridget Young, and Paula R. Williamson, "A Patient and Public Involvement (PPI) Toolkit for Meaningful and Flexible Involvement in Clinical Trials:—A Work in Progress," *Research Involvement and Engagement* 2, no. 1 (2016). https://doi.org/10.1186/s40900-016-0029-8.
20 See CIOMS, *International Ethical Guidelines*; Vibian Angwenyi, "Complex Realities: Community Engagement for a Paediatric Randomized Controlled Malaria Vaccine Trial in Kilifi, Kenya," *Trials* 15, no. 65 (2014): 1–16. https://doi.org/10.1186/1745-6215-15-65; Kate Chatfield, et al., "Research with, Not about, Communities:—Ethical Guidance towards Empowerment in Collaborative Research, a Report for the TRUST Project," *TRUST Project* (July 15, 2018), http://trust-project.eu/wp-content/uploads/2018/07/TRUST-Community-Participation-in-Research-Final.pdf.
21 Okello, et al., "Challenges for Consent and Community Engagement."
22 See TRUST Project, *Global Code of Conduct for Research in Resource-Poor Settings* (2018), www.globalcodeofconduct.org/wp-content/uploads/2018/05/Global-Code-of-Conduct-Brochure.pdf, art. 8, "Respect."
23 Fregonese, "Community Involvement in Biomedical Research."
24 See also Patricia Marshall and Jessica W. Berg, "Protecting Communities in Biomedical Research," *The American Journal of Bioethics* 6, no. 3 (2006): 28–30. https://doi.org/10.1080/15265160600685770; MacQueen, et al., "Evaluating Community Engagement."
25 Fregonese, "Community Involvement in Biomedical Research."
26 Paulina Tindana, et al., "Grand Challenges in Global Health: Community Engagement in Research in Developing Countries," *PLoS Medicine* 4, no. 9 (2007). https://doi.org/10.1371/journal.pmed.0040273; MacQueen, et al., "Evaluating Community Engagement."
27 Claire Leonie Ward, et al., "Good Collaborative Practice: Reforming Capacity Building Governance of International Health Research Partnerships," *Globalization and Health* 14, no. 1 (2018). https://doi.org/10.1186/s12992-017-0319-4.
28 CIOMS, *International Ethical Guidelines*.

29 World Health Organization, *Community Engagement Framework for Quality, People-Centred and Resilient Health Services* (Geneva: World Health Organization, 2017), https://apps.who.int/iris/bitstream/handle/10665/259280/WHO-HIS-SDS-2017.15-eng.pdf.
30 European Group on Ethics in Science and New Technologies, *Ethical Aspects of Clinical Research*, par. 1.25.
31 Palazzani, *Innovation in Scientific Research*.
32 CIOMS, *International Ethical Guidelines*, Guideline 7.
33 Johannes J. van Delden and Rieke van der Graaf, "Revised CIOMS International Ethical Guidelines for Health-Related Research Involving Humans," *JAMA* 317, no. 2 (2017): 135. https://doi.org/10.1001/jama.2016.18977.
34 CIOMS, *International Ethical Guidelines*, Commentary on Guideline 7.
35 Ward, "Good Collaborative Practice."
36 CIOMS, *International Ethical Guidelines*, Commentary on Guideline 9.
37 See World Medical Association, *Declaration of Helsinki* (1964), last version 2013, www.wma.net/policies-post/wma-declaration-of-helsinki-ethical-principles-for-medical-research-involving-human-subjects/, art. 25, and UNESCO, *Universal Declaration on Bioethics and Human Rights* (2005), http://portal.unesco.org/en/ev.php-URL_ID=31058&URL_DO=DO_TOPIC&URL_SECTION=201.html, art. 6.3.
38 Marshall and Berg, "Protecting Communities in Biomedical Research."
39 *Ibid*.
40 National Institutes of Health (NIH)—Clinical and Translational Science Awards Consortium, Community Engagement Key Function Committee, Task Force on the Principles of Community Engagement, *Principles of Community Engagement*, 2nd ed. (2011), www.atsdr.cdc.gov/communityengagement/pdf/PCE_Report_508_FINAL.pdf.
41 Wellcome Trust, *Community Engagement*.
42 NIH, *Principles of Community Engagement*.
43 Browne, "The Willingness to Participate in Biomedical Research."
44 European Medicines Agency, *Reflection Paper on Ethical and GCP Aspects of Clinical Trials of Medicinal Products for Human Use Conducted in Third Countries and Submitted in Marketing Authorisation Applications to the E.M.A.* (2010), www.ema.europa.eu/en/documents/regulatory-procedural-guideline/draft-reflection-paper-ethical-good-clinical-practice-aspects-clinical-trials-medicinal-products_en.pdf; CIOMS, *International Ethical Guidelines*.
45 Chatfield et al., "Research with, Not about, Communities."
46 Patricia Marshall, "Ethical Challenges in Study Design and Informed Consent for Health Research in Resource-Poor Settings," UNICEF/UNDP/World Bank/WHO Special Programme for Research and Training in Tropical Diseases & World Health Organization, https://apps.who.int/iris/bitstream/handle/10665/43622/9789241563383_eng.pdf;sequence=1, accessed May 17, 2021; CIOMS, *International Ethical Guidelines*.
47 Angwenyi, "Complex Realities."
48 Olubukola T. Idoko, et al., "Community Perspectives Associated with the African PsA-TT (MenAfriVac) Vaccine Trials," *Clinical Infectious Diseases* 61, no. suppl. 5 (2015). https://doi.org/10.1093/cid/civ596.
49 National Institute for Health and Care Excellence (NICE), *Community Engagement: Improving Health and Well-Being and Reducing Health Inequalities* (2016), http://nice.org.uk/guidance/ng44.

50 World Health Organization, *Risk Communication and Community Engagement Preparedness and Readiness Framework: Ebola Response in the Democratic Republic of Congo in North Kivu* (2018), www.who.int/iris/handle/10665/275389, where a helpful checklist is provided.
51 Syed Ahmed and Ann-Gel Palermo, "Community Engagement in Research: Frameworks for Education and Peer Review," *American Journal of Public Health* 100, no. 8 (2010): 1380–1387 provide several educational strategies for research team about community engagement—usually traditional doctoral and master's programs do not train specifically on these aspects during researchers' education.
52 Bruce Jennings, "Reconceptualizing Autonomy: A Relational Turn in Bioethics," *Hastings Center Report*, 46 (2016): 11–16.
53 Jennings, "Reconceptualizing Autonomy"; Edward S. Dove, et al., "Beyond Individualism: Is There a Place for Relational Autonomy in Clinical Practice and Research?," *Clinical Ethics* 12, no. 3 (2017): 150–165. https://doi.org/10.1177/1477750917704156; Palazzani, *Innovation in Scientific Research*; Federico De Montalvo Jääskeläinen, *Menores De Edad y Consentimiento Informado* (Valencia: Tirant Lo Blanc, 2019); Silvina Alvarez Medina, *La autonomía de las personas. Una capacidad relacional* (Madrid: Centro de Estudios Políticos y Constitucionales, 2018).
54 The Italian Committee for Bioethics, *Opinion on Migration and Health* (2017), http://bioetica.governo.it/en/opinions/opinions-responses/migration-and-health/.
55 Jennings, "Reconceptualizing Autonomy."
56 Dove, et al., "Beyond Individualism."
57 See Peter I. Osuji, "Relational Autonomy in Informed Consent (RAIC) as an Ethics of Care Approach to the Concept of Informed Consent," *Medicine, Health Care and Philosophy* 21, no. 1 (2017): 101–111. https://doi.org/10.1007/s11019-017-9789-7, where a relational view of autonomy in the informed consent process is grounded on an ethics of care.

4 Healthcare decision-making

Cross-cultural analysis of the shift from the autonomous to the relational self

Joseph Tham and Marie Catherine Letendre

Introduction

Important healthcare decisions in life focus our attention on questions like: Who should I consult? What shall I do? Since health is prized as a prime value, healthcare decision-making necessarily involves consultation and a course of action that offers benefit and reduces harm. In the West, the physician has traditionally exercised the role of principal medical decision-maker. Yet, before the significant medical and scientific advances of the twentieth century, clinical medicine had limited powers to change the health status of individuals with chronic or incurable conditions. Paradoxically, therefore, patient participation in medical decision-making became a greater reality as medicine's powers and scope expanded exponentially, with greater attention now focused on providing information and gaining the patient's consent.

Re-conceptualizing the physician–patient relationship

We can attempt only a very brief historical summary of the events that led to greater patient autonomy here. Various authors have already written differing accounts of how this phenomenon developed as medical ethics took on a new scrutiny, and the multidisciplinary field termed bioethics emerged to deal with moral problems linked to implementing medical, biological and technological advances.[1]

The decisive event following World War II was the Nuremberg trial of 23 Nazi physicians who had conducted experiments on non-consenting prisoners. The resulting Nuremburg Code of 1947 required medical professionals to gain voluntary consent from persons involved in scientific research as well as to adequately inform them of risks and harms.

In the 1950s, before informed consent became known, Szasz and Hollender proposed three models for a more mobile physician–patient relationship that included a range of possibilities to fit the clinical situation and included

DOI: 10.4324/9781003213215-6

participation in healthcare decisions.[2] This may be considered a significant aspect of the discernible shift occurring in clinical medicine in regard to patients being granted a decision-making status. Szasz and Hollender's model of mutual participation acknowledged that "the patient's own experiences provide reliable and important clues for therapy." This model of the doctor–patient relationship involved a process of change the physician had to undergo to have a mutually constructive experience with the patient. Their analysis highlights certain necessary characteristics for a more highly developed relationship in the modern clinical context.

Spurred on by the rights movements of the 1960s, changes in medical decision-making characterized a decade animated by political, religious and social unrest. Scholars from several fields, namely, moral theology and religious studies as well as medicine, law and biology, became increasingly involved in medical ethical issues. Henry K. Beecher published a paper in the *New England Journal of Medicine*, "Ethics and Clinical Research" (1966) in which he outlined 22 real cases of unethical human experimentation.[3] This and other scandals generated a great deal of uproar among the public and the government reacted by commissioning specialists in ethics to come up with guidelines which eventually included the standards of informed consent.

By the 1970s, bioethics emerged to seriously address a number of critical issues brought on by technology and human experimentation. The Belmont Report resulted from an examination of ethical principles and intended to apply guidelines for informed consent, risk–benefit assessment and selections of subjects. The four principles of biomedical ethics, autonomy, beneficence, non-maleficence and justice, provided a theoretical framework for practical decision-making.[4] Principlism, as it came to be known, was routinely praised as often as it was thoroughly criticized. Despite the intent of the four principles to carry equal ethical importance in balancing judgements, autonomy appeared to triumph over the other principles.[5]

The paternalistic perspective of *deciding for* patients and assuming a decision in their best interest gave way to the "contractual" perspective of *discussing with* the patient.[6] Informing the patient adequately and gaining his consent for treatment in the end often meant accepting his decisions without questions as if it were only a business contract. In bioethical practice, patient autonomy received great applause for respecting individual rights and subsequently important legal support (Patient Self-determination Act 1990). The intent to involve patients and respect their autonomy became new terrain for both physicians and patients. Informing and not informing were two sides of the same coin minted as autonomy.

However, there have been conceptual problems with informed consent based exclusively on patient autonomy from the very beginning. For example, if the patient does not want to be involved in decision-making, it is unfair to coerce him/her to make decisions regarding medical care.[7] Moreover, Howard Brody points out that even the contractual model that included the idea of patient autonomy was flawed and incomplete since "what does patient autonomy actually require of a physician?"[8]

To supplant the deficiencies of principlism, physicians, medical ethicists and philosophers offered alternative models that expanded the four principles giving some of the different names.[9]

John Evans noted that the rationalization of bioethical discourse has made it impossible to question what constitutes human good or the ends of medicine. The good of medicine has too often been transformed into meaning the enhancement of self-determination and the pursuit of individual choice. Yet, is ethics possible without the idea of the good? Insofar as bioethics gives its primary attention to crisis issues and the resolution of dilemmas, it undermines the basic presuppositions of medical practice and care. As a result, principlism and its contenders are prone to ever greater moral permissiveness precisely due to the failure of consensus and the employment of secular methodologies.[10]

In the most widely discussed analysis of physician–patient relationships, Emanuel and Emanuel elaborated four models: paternalistic, informative, interpretative and deliberative.[11] As thorough as they may seem, these models do not correspond well with clinical experience since further analysis reveals a pattern of inconsistency in patients' attitudes and behaviours. The search for a model or a set of models to address the complexity of the contemporary patient–physician relationship became historically untenable. The answer to dilemmas involving informed consent, truth-telling or confidentiality does not lie simply with having a workable model.[12] An integrative approach and new communication skills provide a better basis.

In recent years, new treatments for cancer patients necessitated talking with the patient, gaining their consent and assisting the patient in the pursuit of his/her understanding of their best interest. Though patients want to and need to receive information to give consent, the actual choice could always be that they may hand over the decision-making to the physician and/or to their family. Thus, fully informing may result in carefully delegating.

The focus on patient–physician communication, one of the key attributes of patient-centred care,[13] involves breaking bad news better,[14] finding a balance between physician power and patient choice[15] and becoming culturally competent to provide appropriate healthcare.[16] The large influx of immigrants to the United States in the 1980s and 1990s also precipitated a more substantial shift in practice: a set of skills termed cultural competency. At the same time, there was a demographic change in the medical profession going from a profession composed almost entirely of white men to one with significant numbers of men and women from racial minorities.[17] All these factors provide fertile ground to re-examine the role of autonomy in patient's decision-making and informed consent.

Enhanced autonomy as patient participation

In his book, *The Theory and Practice of Autonomy*, Gerald Dworkin describes personal autonomy as self-rule that is free from both the controlling interference by others and from limitations, such as inadequate understanding, that prevent meaningful choice.[18] Acting freely is the essential element of autonomy. However, a construct of respect for autonomy needs neither to be overly individualistic and excessively focused on reason nor unduly legalistic.[19] In applying this construct of respect for the patient's autonomy, the contemporary clinical dialogue necessarily focuses on the significance of talk. The past decade has witnessed a shift in application towards patient-centred approaches to healthcare delivery. A patient-centred approach is basically humanistic and "puts a strong focus on patient participation in clinical decision-making by taking into account the patients' perspective, and tuning medical care to the patients' needs and preferences."[20] The exponential growth in research addressing the nature, dynamics, contexts and consequences of the medical dialogue indicates a twofold benefit: personally rewarding since it is relationship-centred and optimally effective due to importance given to the value of human relationships.[21]

Since free will is an attribute of rational human beings, the notion of autonomy is universally valid. Both internal and external experiences and resources contribute to one's autonomy since from the beginning of our lives, all of us are embedded in a context of social relations that sustain and shape us. The majority of physicians now agree that patient autonomy is actually a complex concept referring to both one's capacity to choose and one's ability to implement one's choices.[22] A person may not always be able to exercise one or both of these aspects. Conditions can and do arise that necessitate delegating another, that is, family member, friend or even a physician, to be the decision-maker.

In this context, autonomy is more correctly described as relational, rather than merely a matter of individual choice. The term *relational autonomy* does not refer to a single unified conception of autonomy, but it is rather an umbrella term designating a range of related perspectives.[23] These perspectives are based on a shared conviction that persons are socially embedded, and their identities are formed by social relationships and shaped by complex social determinants such as race, class, gender and ethnicity. An understanding of the notion of *relational self* serves to frame the ethics of both informed consent issues and truth-telling dilemmas. A reasonable approach is to begin from a basis of unity (i.e. realizing that the person is embedded in a network of intimate relationships) and move outward to understand different approaches that reflect the same reality (i.e. eliciting personal worries and negotiating a decision-making process). The beneficent intention of deciding in favour of the good can be represented in a variety of ways based on the medium of cultural norms and different medical traditions.[24] The physician, the individual patient and the family now all share, in varying degrees, the decisional aspects of healthcare. For medical professionals as well as families, this discernible shift in practice signifies both challenge and opportunity.

This new modality is linked to a strong emphasis on patient autonomy in the doctor–patient relationship and the overwhelming lack of data that receiving bad news significantly impacts patient outcomes in treatment. The bioethical norm of respect for persons is embodied in the notion of autonomy. Drs. Back and Curtis noted in their study that the determination of the type of news that is judged to be bad constitutes a subjective judgement in the mind of the receiver, so when physicians assume that they are delivering bad news, they may influence patients' responses.[25] Several studies have documented that a large majority of both healthy adults and cancer patients from different countries want to be told about their diagnosis and prognosis.[26] Skilled use of cross-cultural understanding and communication techniques increases the likelihood that both the process and outcomes of care are satisfactory for all involved. Studies in truth-telling and cultural differences reveal another important aspect, namely, dealing with culturally relevant bioethics.[27] The move towards an interpretative cross-cultural bioethics indicates that plurality of reasonable decision-making possibilities does exist alongside each other.[28]

Cross-cultural aspects of healthcare

Culture, which encompasses beliefs and behaviours that are learned and shared by members of a social group, fundamentally shapes how individuals construct meaning out of particular life events. Explanations for disease, illness, suffering and dying contribute to the cultural basis for confronting these events. The power of cultural identity can hardly be overestimated. With increased diversity in the United States, many European countries and Australia, encounters between patients and physicians of different backgrounds are becoming more common. Cultural diversity is on the increase worldwide as immigration, travel and the global economy make national borders more permeable. It is estimated that in the United States by the year 2050, minorities will make up 47% of the population.[29] The challenge for clinicians in an increasingly diverse society is met by understanding the cultural factors that influence patients' responses to such issues as healing, suffering, chemically-based medications, genetic predispositions, the stigma associated with certain conditions and life-threatening ailments.

Thus, the risk for cross-cultural misunderstandings surrounding care at the end of life is also increasing.[30] Studies have shown significant cultural differences in attitudes towards truth-telling, life-prolonging technology and decision-making styles at the end of life. A new set of skills in cultural competency has been developed as an effort to improve health outcomes.[31]

Cultural competence for the physician would involve *learning about* the patient's preferences and ethnic background. However, this is easier said than done. For instance, implementing procedures that require informed consent, a tangible proof of respecting individual choice, proved very difficult due to the patient or the family's expectations of being shielded from the truth of an incurable condition.[32] In other cases, the notion of signing a piece of paper for healthcare services could be foreign and disrespectful.[33] Ethnicity shades the attitudes of many patients and, therefore, re-shapes patient autonomy and consent.[34] Ethnic groups brought with them cultural views of healthcare and a paradigm of the physician/patient relationship that frequently called in question the notion of universality of the four bio-ethical principles.

The ethical concerns and experiences of clinical practice tested bioethics as it met diverse cultural perspectives at the crossroads of the twentieth-century biomedicine. Multiculturalists state that physicians, patients and their families can inhabit distinctively different social worlds and may be guided by diverse understandings of moral practice.[35] The concepts of *medicine* and *healing* have definitions rooted in a myriad of cultural aspects: accumulated observation and writings, attitudes about health and illness, diverse medicinal approaches that are either natural or chemical and most recently in scientific-technological advances.[36] Communication between patient and physician is more aptly associated with patients' perceptions of finding common ground with their physicians and trusting them and with improved health outcomes.[37] Therefore, the enormous force of cultural viewpoints and the contemporary transformation of the physician/patient relationship in accommodating bioethical principles and gaining cultural competence mark a new step in shared decision-making.[38] Cultural competency in the clinician's skill set becomes an asset in dealing with the aspects of care rooted in cultural differences and knowledge of the fact that a person of a particular ethnic background may not subscribe to his/her cultural medical tradition is foundational.

The important factor in becoming culturally competent is the understanding of how culture does influence a clinical relationship and not to over-emphasize cultural difference and fall prey to the mistaken idea that if the cultural root of the problem can be identified then the problem will be solved. The situation will always be more much complicated.[39] In the United States, the socio-cultural differences between patient and physician influence communication and clinical decision-making. Language proficiency, the probable need for interpreters, acknowledging possible issues of mistrust and the impact of culture on discussing negative information form a significant part of mastering cultural competency.[40] The downstream effect of such competency would be greater trust, fewer gaps, "moral growth, and a strengthening of fundamental professional commitments."[41]

Cultural norms specify behaviour. "Honesty is an ideal value for most Americans, but it varies in strength as a real value for other cultures."[42] Honour is highly prized in the Japanese culture as is female purity in the Islamic world. Direct eye contact is avoided in several cultures, notably Asian and the Middle Eastern culture; the Navaho use silence to formulate their thoughts to give the most complete answer. Trust is given only to family members in the Gypsy culture. Masculine and feminine pronouns do not exist in Asian languages, and "yes" does not always mean the affirmative since many cultures use the "yes" as a way of avoiding an embarrassing "no." This is just a shortlist of cultural variables that inform and form communication styles. A cross-cultural healthcare ethic combines the tenets of patient- and family-centred care with an understanding of the social and cultural influences that affect the quality of medical services and treatment. Developing sensitivity to different cultures can make healthcare programs and activities attractive and interesting for a broader population base. In contrast, a lack of cultural sensitivity can deter people from using healthcare services.

The task of developing a richer understanding of the patient's preferences becomes the fulcrum for integrating responsible choices in healthcare. In short, cultural competency on the part of the physician becomes capacity building for the patient. Knowledge of another's cultural context is experienced as respect. This is human service of the highest order. Intercultural respect, therefore, has direct relevance for healthcare ethics since in the healthcare setting personal decisions and actions need to be consistent with values, beliefs and decision-making customs.[43] Oftentimes, the family's role does, indeed, favour the best interests of the patient. The patient needs the information to make plans, select treatment options and include the family in providing and sustaining care as is traditionally done in communitarian societies such as China.[44]

Clinicians, who possess a skilful use of patient-centred questions, demonstrate an interest in cultural heritage and are able to appraise the family's role in decision-making assist effectively in shared decision-making. While offering autonomy to patients, cultural norms are respected while rights to decisions displaying "a relational self" are simultaneously acknowledged. The patient who refuses diagnostic information and prefers family- and physician-centred decision-making has made a clear, voluntary choice.[45] Physicians who care for patients with life-threatening conditions should discuss with them the extent to which they wish to involve their families in decisions at the end of life. To practice medicine according to a shared decision-making model, physicians need to offer more explicit information, explore patients' values and beliefs regarding serious illnesses and respect their wishes throughout treatment.[46]

Even though a patient desires a shared decision-making style that includes the family, a family member may fear being blamed for providing inadequate care by other family members: in this instance, the physician's role in providing care will be to mediate the conflict.[47] Further study will be needed as the occurrence of a patient's view of the relational self intersects with concordance in family participation in decision-making generally and in particular at the end of life. Further research is needed to design a communitarian paradigm of patient and family with the physician that helps patients make free decisions despite the burdens that their illnesses may bring.[48] In the case of surrogate decision-makers, research indicates that most surrogates of critically ill patients do not view withholding prognostic information as an acceptable way to maintain hope.[49] Timely discussions help all members to prepare emotionally and existentially for the possibility of death. As the current trend in shared decision-making represents, the shift from individual to relational self marks a significant step in the journey towards a richer understanding of the self both in relation to the preferred role and in the level of involvement.

Conclusion

A considerable distance has been covered in the past 40 years of medical decision-making. The so-called doctor knows best approach was abandoned in favour of a newer approach that respected the patient's autonomy to consent for treatment and therapies through dialogue. However, an excessive emphasis on individual self-determination and autonomy was also considered inhuman and unsatisfactory. As soon as the patient was involved in medical decision-making, the importance of sharing those decisions with family or deferring to the physician also became a reality.[50]

Lately, cultural diversity has challenged the assumption of common meaning. More importantly, it highlighted the need for broad understanding since a narrowly defined view of patient autonomy and a restricting application of the principle of informed consent in a cultural context produce adverse effects.[51] The prevailing evidence of research brings to light a considerable variation in patients' preferences for participation and role in decision-making.[52] A culturally relevant approach advocated by bioethicists for medical decision-making relies on seeking an understanding of cultural diversity and exploring its complexity;[53] in fact, medical practice has specific cultural paradigms.[54]

Simply deciding in the best interests of the patient has developed into a complex field of choices: the preferred role, the degree of participation, the varying stages of seeking help and the ability to determine the appropriate timing for shared decision-making. Responsibility and deliberation bear especially on professional doctoring since situations of conflict may accompany decision-making and consent gaining in biomedicine.[55]

The shift in the West from individual autonomy to relational autonomy in medical decision-making invites new reflections on respecting personal dignity and identity. The words of Michelangelo, after he had already accomplished so much, "*Sto ancora imparando*" (And still I am learning), captures the momentum and focuses our attention on the needs of the human person as a relational self. It is not possible to equalize the ability to decide autonomously and the reality of implementing a healthcare decision that, of necessity, involves others. The objectivity of early conceptions of autonomy conflicts with the "subjective" dimensions currently experienced as the patients' opinions on treatment, the effects a disease process has on the context of relationships and the numerous issues related to this framing of individual and collective experiences.

Admittedly, the indisputable achievement of the principle of autonomy gave shape to human identity. However, without the notion of relational autonomy, the design of human identity is incomplete. Relational autonomy affords both objectivity and subjectivity since it responds to and interprets the deeper sensibilities of the human person. The next step in achieving the shift would require a change of point of view, and not of language. To embrace the model of the relational self would improve practice and move the issue of shared decision-making to a broader and important context.

Acknowledgement

Originally published as S. Joseph Tham and Marie Catherine Letendre, "Healthcare Decision-Making: Cross-cultural Analysis of the Shift from the Autonomous to the Relational Self," *The New Bioethics* 20.2 (2014), 174–185. http://essential.metapress.com/content/t5n363u29567k101/.

Notes

1 David Rothman, *Strangers at the Bedside: A History of How Law and Bioethics Transformed Medical Decision Making* (New York: Harpers Collins, 1991);

Elio Sgreccia, *Personalist Bioethics* (Philadelphia: National Catholic Bioethics Center, 2012), 3–29; Albert Jonsen, *The Birth of Bioethics* (New York: Oxford University Press, 1988); Rene Fox and Judith Swazey, *Observing Bioethics* (New York: Oxford University Press, 2008), 21–73.
2 Thomas Szasz and Marc Hollender, "The Basic Models of the Doctor-Patient Relationship," in *The Social Medicine Reader* (Durham, NC: Duke University Press, 1952), 279–286. The authors discuss three models: Model One-Activity-Passivity in which treatment takes place irrespective of the patient's contribution and regardless of the outcome; Model Two-Guidance & Cooperation in which both persons are active in that they contribute to the relationship but the main difference pertains to power and to its actual or potential use; Model Three-Mutual Participation in which the doctor helps the patient help himself/herself and a partnership emerges.
3 Henry K. Beecher, "Ethics and Clinical Research," *New England Journal of Medicine*, 274, no. 27 (1966): 367–372.
4 Tom Beauchamp and James Childress, *Principles of Biomedical Ethics* (New York: Oxford University Press, 1979).
5 Paul Wolpe, "The Triumph of Autonomy in American Bioethics: A Sociological View," in *Bioethics and Society: Constructing the Ethical Enterprise*, ed. Raymond DeVries and Janardan Subedi (Upper Saddle River, NJ: Prentice-Hall, 1998), 38–59.
6 Donald Oken, "What to Tell Cancer Patients: A Study of Medical Attitudes," *Journal of the American Medical Association* 175 (1961): 1120–1128; D.H. Novack, et al., "Changes in Physicians' Attitudes towards Telling the Cancer Patient," *Journal of the American Medical Association* 241, no. 9 (1979): 897–900.
7 David E. Ost, "The 'Right' Not to Know," *Journal of Medicine and Philosophy* 9, no. 3 (1984): 301–312.
8 Howard Brody, "Transparency: Informed Consent in Primary Care," *Hastings Center Report* 19, no. 5 (1989): 5–9. Dr. Brody favours a "transparency standard" under which physicians explain the thinking behind their selection of treatment and then encourages patients to ask questions. Informed consent is achieved if a patient agrees to a treatment after thinking has been made transparent. Rather than having to list every possible risk a "reasonable patient" might wish to know to make a decision, physicians would be legally responsible only for explaining their own reasoning.
9 Lynn Payer, *Medicine and Culture: Varieties of Treatment in the United States, England, West Germany and France* (New York: Henry Holt and Co., 1988), 15–34; Edmund Pellegrino and David Thomasma, *The Virtues in Medical Practice* (New York: Georgetown University Press, 1996); Dan English, *Bioethics: A Clinical Guide for Medical Students* (New York: W.W. Norton and Company, 1994); H. Tristram Engelhardt, Jr., *The Foundations of Bioethics* (New York: Oxford University Press, 1996); Robert Veatch, "Abandoning Informed Consent," *Hastings Center Report* 25, no. 2 (1995): 5–12; Robert Veatch, "Doctor Does Not Know Best: Why in the New Century Physicians Must Stop Trying to Benefit Patients," *Journal of Medicine and Philosophy* 25, no. 6 (2000): 701–721.
10 John Evans J., *Playing God? Human Genetic Engineering and Its Rationalization of Public Bioethical Debate* (Chicago: University of Chicago Press, 2000); S. Joseph Tham, *The Secularization of Bioethics: A Critical History*, Doctoral Dissertation (Rome: UPRA Press, 2007).

11 Ezekiel Emanuel and Linda Emanuel, "Four Models of the Physician/Patient Relationship," *Journal of American Medical Association* 267, no. 16 (1992): 2221–2227. The authors defined the models as follows:

> *paternalistic:* physician makes decisions for the patient's benefit independent of patient's values and desires;
> *informative:* physician provides information, patient applies values and decides;
> *interpretative:* patient is uncertain about values, physician, as counsellor, assists the patient in elucidating values;
> *deliberative:* patient is open to development; physician teaches desirable values. Emanuel and Emanuel argue in favour of the deliberative model, seeing the others as exceptions to the norm that require justification.

12 Greg Clarke, Robert T. Hall, and Greg Rosencrance, "Physician-Patient Relations: No More Models," *American Journal of Bioethics* 4, no. 2 (2004): 16–19. The authors cite in their research that there was no significant correlation between patients wanting to make the decision to be put on a ventilator and their having legally appointed a surrogate and mention other inconsistencies with regard to medical decision making that one would expect most patients to be able to make. Their research indicates that there appears to be considerable variety in patient preferences for decision models, so the search for a single best model is based on a misguided assumption that one protocol fits all clinical situations or even may fit all situations.

13 Eric Cassell, *Talking with Patients*, Vol. 1: *The Theory of Doctor-Patient Communication* (Cambridge: MIT Press, 1985).

14 Robert Buckman and Yvonne Kason, *How to Break Bad News: A Guide for Professionals* (Baltimore, MD: John Hopkins University Press, 1992).

15 Timothy E. Quill and Howard Brody, "Physician Recommendations and Patient Autonomy: Finding a Balancing between Physician Power and Patient Choice," *Annals of Internal Medicine* 125, no. 9 (1996): 763–769.

16 Joseph A. Carrese and Lorna A. Rhodes, "Western Bioethics on the Navajo Reservation," *Journal of the American Medical Association* 274, no. 10 (1995): 826–829.

17 Arnold S. Relman, "Here Come the Women," *New England Journal of Medicine* 302, no. 22 (1980): 1252–1253; C. Eisenberg, "Medicine Is No Longer a Man's Profession: Or, When the Men's Club Goes Coed It's Time to Change the Regs," *New England Journal of Medicine* 321, no. 22 (1989): 1542–1547.

18 Gerald Dworkin, *The Theory and Practice of Autonomy* (Cambridge: Cambridge University Press, 1988).

19 Tom Beauchamp and James Childress, *Principles of Biomedical Ethics*, 5th ed. (New York: Oxford University Press, 2001).

20 Jozien Bensing, "Bridging the Gap: The Separate Worlds of Evidence Based Medicine and Patient Centered Medicine," *Patient Education and Counseling* 39, no. 1 (2000): 17–25.

21 Debra Roter and Judith Hall, *Doctors Talking with Patients / Patients Talking to Doctors*, 2nd ed. (Westport, CT: Praeger, 2006).

22 Antonella Surbone, "Telling the Truth to Patients with Cancer: What Is the Truth?," *Lancet Oncology* 7, no. 11 (2006): 994–950.

23 Historically, Jennifer Nedelsky was the first person to specify the concept of *relational autonomy* from an explicitly feminist perspective. Jennifer Nedelsky,

"Re-Conceiving Autonomy: Sources, Thoughts and Possibilities," *Yale Journal of Law and Feminism* 1 (1989): 7–36; Catriona MacKenzie and Natalie Stoljar, *Relational Autonomy* (New York: Oxford University Press, 2000), 3–31.
24 Marie-Catherine Letendre, *The Bioethical and Cultural Implications of the Truth-Telling Debates*, Doctoral Dissertation, Ateneo Pontificio Regina Apostolorum (Rome: IF Press, 2010).
25 Anthony L. Back and J. Randall Curtis, "Communicating Bad News," *Western Journal of Medicine* 176, no. 3 (2002): 177–180.
26 Jung Kwak and William E. Haley, "Current Research Findings on End-of-Life Decision Making among Racially or Ethnically Diverse Groups," *The Gerontologist* 45, no. 5 (2005): 634–641.
27 Mark Kuczewski and Patrick J. McCruden, "Informed Consent: Does It Take a Village? The Problem of Culture and Truth-Telling," *Cambridge Quarterly of Healthcare Ethics* 10, no. 1 (2001): 34–46.
28 Jing-Bao Nie, "The Plurality of Chinese and American Medical Moralities: Towards an Interpretative Cross-Cultural Bioethics," *Kennedy Institute of Ethics Journal* 10, no. 3 (2000): 239–260.
29 Jean Lau Chin and Judyann Bigby, "The Care of Asian Americans," in *Cross-Cultural Medicine*, ed. Judyann Bigby (Philadelphia, PA: American College of Physicians, 2003), 129–159; Marjorie Kagawa-Singer, et al., "Negotiating Cross-Cultural Issues at the End-of-Life," *JAMA* 286, no. 23 (2001): 3000; Terry L. Cross, et al., *Towards a Culturally Competent System of Care*, Vol. 1, CASSP Technical Assistance Center (Washington, DC: Georgetown University Press, 1989).
30 Russell Searight and Jennifer Gafford, "Cultural Diversity at the End of Life," *American Family Physician* 71, no. 3 (2005): 515–521.
31 Joseph Betancourt, "Cross-Cultural Medical Education: Conceptual Approaches and Frameworks for Evaluation," *Academic Medicine* 78, no. 6 (2005): 560–569.
32 Jessica H. Muller and Brian Desmond, "Ethical Dilemmas in Cross-Cultural Context: A Chinese Example," *The Western Journal of Medicine* 157, no. 3 (1992): 323–327.
33 Geri-Ann Galanti, *Caring for Patients from Different Cultures: Case Studies from American Hospitals* (Philadelphia: University of Pennsylvania Press, 1991).
34 Leslie Blackhall, et al., "Ethnicity and Attitudes towards Patient Autonomy," *Journal of the American Medical Association* 274, no. 10 (1995): 820–825.
35 Engelhardt, *The Foundations of Bioethics*.
36 Rachel E. Spector, *Cultural Diversity in Health and Illness* (Upper Saddle River, NJ: Prentice Hall, 2000).
37 Onora O'Neill, *Autonomy and Trust in Bioethics* (New York: Cambridge University Press, 2002), 118–136.
38 Betancourt, "Cross-Cultural Medical Education . . ."
39 Arthur Kleinman and Peter Benson, "Anthropology in the Clinic: The Problem of Cultural Competency and How to Fix It," *PLoS Med* 3, no. 10 (2006): e294. doi: 10.1371/journal.pmed.0030294.
40 John L. Oliffe, et al, "Truth-Telling and Cultural Assumptions in an Era of Informed Consent," *Family Community Health* 30, no. 1 (2007): 5–15.
41 Y. Michael Barilan, "Responsibility as a Meta-Virtue: Truth-Telling, Deliberation and Wisdom in Medical Professionalism," *Journal of Medical Ethics* 35, no. 3 (2009): 153–158.
42 Spector, *Cultural Diversity in Health and Illness*.

43 Karen Gervais, "Changing Society, Changing Medicine, Changing Bioethics," in *Bioethics and Society*, ed. DeVries and Subedi, 216–232.
44 Ruiping Fan, "Confucian Familism and Its Bioethical Implications," in *The Family Medical Decision-Making, and Biotechnology: Critical Reflections on Asian Moral Perspectives*, ed. Shui Chuen Lee, Vol. 91 (Dordrecht: Springer, 2007), 15–26.
45 Searight and Gafford, "Cultural Diversity at the End of Life."
46 Peter Angelos, Charles Bennett, and Cecilia Tomori, "Communication: From Paternalism to Shared Decision Making," *Oncology News International* 10, no. 2 (2001). www.cancernetwork.com/display/article/10165/97468.
47 Marie T. Nolan, et al., "Family Health Care Decision Making and Self-Efficacy with Patients with ALS at the End of Life," *Palliative Supportive Care* 6, no. 3 (2008): 273–280.
48 Sapana Patel, Suzanne Bakken, and Cornelia Ruland, "Recent Advances in Shared Decision Making for Mental Health," *Current Opinion in Psychiatry* 21, no. 6 (2008): 606–612.
49 Latifat Apatira, et al., "Hope, Truth, and Preparing for Death: Perspectives of Surrogate Decision Makers," *Annals of Internal Medicine* 149, no. 12 (2008): 861–868.
50 Emilia D'Antuono, "Therapeutic Obstinacy: Notes for an Analysis of Endo-of-Life Bioethical Issues," in *Bioethical Issues by the Interuniversity Center for Bioethics Research*, UNESCO Chair in Bioethics 9th World Conference, Bioethics, Medical Ethics and Health Law towards the 21st Century (Naples, Editoriale Scientifica, 2013), 11–26.
51 Oliffe, et al., "Truth-Telling and Cultural Assumptions . . ."
52 Quyen Ngo-Metzger, et al., "End-of-Life Care: Guidelines for Patient Centered Communication," *American Family Physician* 77, no. 2 (2008): 167–174; James Hallenbeck and Robert Arnold, "A Request for Non-Disclosure: Don't Tell Mother," *Journal of Clinical Oncology* 25, no. 31 (2007): 5030–5034.
53 Kuczewski and McCruden, "Informed Consent . . ."; Howard Brody and Linda Hunt, "Moving Beyond Cultural Stereotypes in End-of-Life Decisions," *American Family Physician* 71, no. 3 (2005): 429–430; Leigh Turner, "From the Local to the Global: Bioethics and the Concept of Culture," *Journal of Medicine and Philosophy* 30, no. 3 (2005): 305–320.
54 Payer, *Medicine and Culture* . . .
55 Barilan, "Responsibility as a Meta-Virtue . . ."

Part II
Religious perspectives on informed consent

5 Informed consent
A critical response from a Buddhist perspective

Ellen Y. Zhang

Introduction

According to UNESCO Declaration of Bioethics and Human Rights (UDBHR), informed consent process requires four characteristics to be valid: voluntariness, disclosure, understanding and capacity. Whenever one of these elements is missing, informed consent can be compromised. In their *Principle of Biomedical Ethics*, Tom L. Beauchamp and James F. Childress claim that informed consent is an individual's autonomous authorization. They postulate seven structural elements, including threshold elements (competence to understand and decide; voluntariness in deciding), information elements (disclosure of material information; recommendation of a plan; understanding of the information and recommended plan) and consent elements (decision in favour of the plan; authorization of the chosen plan). In this chapter, I will first look at these four characteristics and then discuss their ethical implications (e.g. individual autonomy and human rights), followed by a critical response of these implications from a perspective of Buddhism.

Voluntariness

Beauchamp and Childress argue that virtually all codes of medical ethics and institutional regulations should require physicians to obtain informed consent from patients before substantial interventions, with the protection of patient autonomy as the primary justification for this requirement. Voluntariness is usually seen as a choice being made from a person's free will instead of coercion or duress. Voluntariness is, as such, closely associated with the protection of a person's autonomy. Such an idea in history can be traced back to *the Nuremberg Code* and *the Declaration of Helsinki* regarding permissible medical experiments.[1] Nowadays, informed consent focuses on both medical treatments and [medical] research projects.[2]

The word "autonomy" is etymologically derived from old Greek and is a compound of the word *autos*, which means "self," and the word *nomos*,

DOI: 10.4324/9781003213215-8

which means "rule" or "governance." Today the word is used in quite diverse meanings. It, thus, does not refer to a univocal concept, as Beauchamp and Childress have put it, "like many philosophical concepts, 'autonomy' acquires a more specific meaning in the context of a theory."[3] Nevertheless, two conditions are essential in terms of the concept of autonomy: (1) liberty (i.e. independence from controlling influences) and (2) agency (i.e. capacity for intentional action). It follows that the idea of "voluntariness" implies that the patient, as an autonomous individual, should be absent from any substantial control by others and that the patient acts intentionally. In addition, Beauchamp and Childress add the third condition, that is, an autonomous agent should have a complete understanding of his/her action. Therefore, voluntariness needs to meet three conditions: liberty, agency and understanding. The basic idea is to respect self-determination concerning the patient's health.

Disclosure

What must a physician disclose to the patient? What does it mean by "permission to disclose"? Disclosure means that the medical professional is obligated to disclose a core set of information to the patient or subject regarding the treatment or research. According to the UDBHR document, "Disclosure means giving subjects all the relevant and right information about the research, including the risks, potential benefits, nature and other therapeutic alternatives.... The principle of autonomy and obligation truth-telling, places disclosure on always providing the complete information to every patient." However, at the same time, the document indicates that based on the principle of beneficence and the principle of non-maleficence, the information disclosed to the patient can be partial. However, the question of "standards of disclosure" or the need for "intentional or deliberate nondisclosure" has by no means been answered without further qualifications. Regarding nondisclosure, for example, Beauchamp and Childress assert four conditions that are essential to justify the use of intentional nondisclosure in medical research: (1) it is essential to obtain vital information; (2) no substantial risk is involved; (3) the subjects are informed that deception is a part of the study and (4) the subjects give their consent to participate under these conditions.[4]

Understanding

Since informed consent emphasizes the autonomous choice as mentioned in the idea of voluntariness, informed consent in this sense "occurs if and only if a patient or subject, with substantial understanding and in substantial absence of control by others, intentionally authorizes a professional to do something."[5] Nevertheless, without understanding the patient's part, or the autonomous subject, information disclosure has no real meaning. However, the idea of "substantial understanding" is a tricky one even if he or she is *adequately* informed since it has a lot to do with the capacity for intentional action and the capacity for grasping the [highly professional] information being disclosed. Therefore, the UDBHR document states that "appropriate, precise and relevant information should be provided in a language and format that patients fully understand (UNESCO 2005)."

Capacity

Capacity is essential in terms of voluntariness and understanding. A patient needs to have the capacity of self-determination to reflect, decide and consider when deciding to participate in a clinical trial or receiving medical treatment. It is also true that "(a)s the importance of the decision increases, and the information given is more specific and accurate, the threshold for considering a patient capable, is also higher." The patient's health literacy level will influence his/her capacity for understanding.

The four characteristics described earlier indicate several key components that link with ethical implications: individual autonomy, the virtue of rationality, human rights and equality, and the latter two are especially implied in the idea of "improving the readability, design and obtaining process of consent forms taking into account the conscious and unconscious bias by the investigator."

Critical responses

A critical response from multiculturalism and interreligious perspectives

Whenever we deal with a dynamic interaction between universal principles and multiculturalism or and interreligious perspectives, we need to acknowledge the complexity of cultural, societal and religious differences. At the same time, we should also recognize the importance of generalization as a tool to understand the existing common ground or overlapping consensus among different cultures, societies and religions.

As a universal principle, informed consent is generally acknowledged as an ethical ideal. Universal recognition of the merits of the principle has in no way been accompanied by a universally accepted definition of it. Take the four characteristics of informed consent, for example. Different cultures may interpret voluntariness, disclosure, understanding and capacity differently. Another example, in Japan, informed consent is understood as "explanation and agreement" (*setsumei to doi*), which may not be the same as giving individuals clear information about alternative treatments and potential risks and benefits, or the patient can make an informed choice. The Chinese translation is "knowing the information and consent" (知情同意), but in its application, both "informed disclosed" and "consent" entail more complex meanings other than what is indicated in the general principle. In China, informed consent sometimes becomes legal protection of the medical professionals rather than one for patients, thus creating arbitrariness of physicians' relation to patients.

Moreover, there are two questions to be considered: 1) the "thin principle" (harm principle or restraining human experiments in medical research, all patients are equal in terms of informed consent) is more likely to be accepted than the "thick principle" (like self-determination, individual's specific rights). 2) The implied cultural clashes (like individualism vs. familism or collectivism). As a result, informed consent is sometimes employed in non-Western cultural contexts without justifying or even spelling out the definition and without selecting empirical measures that match the stipulated (or intended) definition. The thin principle of informed consent comprises the formal or instrumental aspects of the principle. These instruments can be applied in any functioning medical system, regardless of its political or religious ideology, level of democracy or level of liberalism. The thick principle of informed consent, in contrast, incorporates economic systems, forms of traditional values, circumstances of religious faith and interpretations of human rights or duties.

Informed consent has been accepted today as both an ethical and legal binding between medical professionals and patients, yet the clash between the principle of informed consent and traditional (or premodern) values remains—for example, the question of trust. Trust is traditionally favoured in China, which is subjective and often based on human relations. While local culture may shape people's perception over time, people are more likely to trust experts that share a similar tradition with them. However, such trust is challenged by the modern style of hospitals where patients and their family members are often "at the mercy of a stranger." It is a kind of situation many people do not feel comfortable if they are sceptical about the professionalism of their doctors (like the situation in China today). Alternatively, an ethical dilemma arises when (Western trained) medical professionals seeking informed consent have very different values and belief systems from those (very often uneducated) whose consent is being sought.

Ethical unity in the face of cultural diversity has been an issue that needs to be addressed. Globalization in past decades attempted to promote a universal approach to humanity that enables the formation of a "cosmopolitan" community. The idea of "a shared morality" has been accepted to a certain degree. The voice of cultural and religious particularism should be heard as well. Now, I will turn to Buddhism to address bioethical unity in the context of multiculturalism and religious pluralism.

A critical response from Buddhism

Respect for the dignity and autonomy of patients is a fundamental idea of ethical decision-making, which is well reflected in the principle of informed consent. However, such concepts as individual dignity and autonomy and human rights are not derived directly from Buddhist doctrines. Then, how do we understand informed consent from Buddhism?

As my earlier essay on human dignity and human rights has submitted. However, the Buddhist tradition has no language equivalent to "human dignity" or "human rights." It would have no problem accepting the thin concept of human rights, especially when the fundamental right to life is violated or threatened. In other words, human rights are necessary because they reflect certain moral standards of how humans should be treated and how a violation of such standards should be condemned. From this perspective, we can see that UDBHR uses the general concept of human rights "to underline the importance of biodiversity and its conservation as a common concern of humankind."[6] The rights talk implied in informed consent serves the same purpose in that the key idea of informed consent is to protect the patient's interest (endorsed by the principle of beneficence and the principle of non-maleficence). That means Buddhism would accept a qualified notion of human rights as a protective mechanism.

Buddhism would be very cautious about using the rights language since human rights suggested in informed consent is used as a means not only to protect individuals but also to affirm "moral individualism." Although people talk about collective rights, that is, the rights of a particular group or community (such as children's, women's and gay rights), the idea of human rights, whether positive or negative, is based on free-standing individuals and individual autonomy. From the perspective of Buddhism, "invoking rights has the inevitable effect of emphasizing individuals and their status, thereby strengthening the illusion of self. While Buddhism has a holistic view of life, the rights perspective is essentially atomistic."[7]

As voluntariness is based on autonomy, it requires two conditions: liberty or freedom to choose an agent's capacity for intentional action. Nevertheless, if we scrutinize these two conditions from Buddhism, we will find them somehow ambivalent. Autonomy means self-determination, self-governance or choosing without the controlling influence of others. However, the question is how "the controlling influence of others" be defined.

According to the Buddhist doctrine of (inter)dependent-origination, absolute self-determination is impossible since "self" is causally produced by "others," particularly in cultures like China and Japan, where the self cannot be fully defined without an adequate understanding of the family dynamics. In the case of informed consent, it is very often difficult for physicians (and patients) to determine if a patient's deferral of decision-making is his/her own choice or the result of formative influences of the family. It follows that the patient's capacity for intentional action is also questionable. Voluntariness involves the idea of "free will," which would be problematic for Buddhists, and medical decision-making based entirely on patient-centred orientation would be problematic for Buddhists.

Autonomy is at the core of human agency in Western philosophy. Reconceptualization of autonomy as "personal" autonomy" enables persons to be self-governing in their personal lives.[8] Let us talk about autonomy as self-determination and self-governance first. The self in Buddhism can be understood in two ways: self in the ultimate reality (*paramarthasa*) and self in the conventional reality (*samvrtisat*). From the perspective of ultimate reality, the self is an illusion and an impossibility due to the nature of impermanence. From the perspective of the conventional reality, the "self" has no substance or "self-nature" due to the nature of dependent origination of all things. The Buddhist concept of *anatman* (usually translated as "no-self") denies the notion of a unitary, unchanging self or the idea of self-identification and self-sufficiency. In other words, Buddhism questions the ontological/epistemological reality of the self.

According to the Buddhist tradition, what is conceived as an individual consists of five types of aggregates (*skandhas*) that serve as the bases of designating persons or personhood: (1) material form or body (*rūpa*); (2) sensations (*vedanā*); (3) apperception or perception (*saṃjña*); (4) volitions or mental formations (*saṃskāra*) and (5) consciousness (*vijñāna*). Although various Buddhist schools interpret the five aggregates in somewhat different ways, they all agree that the self has something to do with the phenomenon of self-consciousness and self-identification. The early Buddhist teaching on no-self is recorded in a well-known dialogue between Greco-Bactrian King Milinda and a Buddhist sage named Nagasena. The latter uses the metaphor of chariot to explicate the idea of self or personhood. Nagasena asked whether the collection of all these objects could be called the chariot (picture them piled up together). The king replied, "No." Nagasena then asked whether the chariot could be found *outside* that collection of objects, and the answer was no. The dialogue then continued as follows:

NAGASENA: "Then, ask as I may, I can discover no chariot at all. Just a mere sound is this 'chariot.' But what is the real chariot? Your Majesty has told a lie, has spoken a falsehood! There really is no chariot . . ." Milinda: "I have not, Nagasena, spoken a falsehood. For it is independence on the pole, the axle, the wheels, the framework, the flag-staff, etc., that there takes place this denomination 'chariot,' this designation, this conceptual term, a current appellation, and a mere name."

NAGASENA: "Your Majesty has spoken well about the chariot. It is just so with me. In dependence on the thirty-two parts of the body and the five aggregates (*skandhas*) there takes place this denomination 'Nagasena,' this designation, this conceptual term, a current appellation, and a mere name. In ultimate reality, however, this person cannot be apprehended."[9]

The point here is not that there is no chariot, but there no chariot-hood, or totality of chariot outside that collection of objects, that is, the pole, the axle, the wheels, the framework, the flag-staff, yoke, reins and so on. Likewise, there is no "absolute," "enduring" and "permanent" self that is perceived as "personhood" that goes beyond the five principles components of a human being, that is, the interdependent aggregates which are not fixed and in constant change themselves. Therefore, we read:

Nothing is permanent. The illusion of permanence causes suffering.
The everlasting self is impermanent.
Clinging to the false notion that an enduring self exists increases suffering.[10]

The question of "who or what am I" is, then, answered by the notion of a causally dependent self rather than an enduring self. It follows that "self" in self-identification and self-determination cannot be absolutely atomic and autonomous. From a psychological perspective, an individual's self-consciousness is dependent on the "psychophysical continua" that form the momentary usage of the term "self."[11] What one has experienced that arrives at a sense of continuous self-awareness is nothing but "a bundle of successive impressions or perceptions" if we borrow an expression from David Hume. Nevertheless, the bundle of experiences one has is not, according to Buddhism, a *random* collection of experiences in any case; instead, one is in a particular kind of collection brought about by a particular set of causes and effects. As Nagasena's metaphor demonstrates, there is a certain kind of reality to the "self," just as there is a reality to a chariot. Along this line of thinking, voluntariness is determined by looking at the totality of the circumstances rather than an individual-centred reality or merely the idea of self-determination. What one considers the "I" is in actuality "certain clusters of physical and mental events" linked causally dependent arising.[12]

As for the patient's capacity for intentional action, Buddhism promotes meditative practice that will enable the agent to understand his/herself fully. Buddhism pays special attention to intention as a mental designation, as any action is influenced by intentionality, which is determined by how the mind perceives things. For Buddhists, intentional action is a rational decision yet cannot be reduced to physical mechanisms. The Buddhist concept "karma" also means "intentional action." As it said, "I am the owner of my actions (karma), heir to my actions, born of my actions, related through my actions, and have my actions as my arbitrator" (*Aṅguttara Nikāya*, 5, 57). The Buddhist idea here is that one should take responsibility for one's actions.

Nevertheless, the question is whether the patient identified in informed consent has the capacity for intentional action. Let us not talk about external influences by others, but how about internal influences when the agent is confronting a life-and-death situation. Can we expect a patient to be always rational enough so that he/she can fully understand his/her intention? That is why the Buddhists recommend meditation, and the practice of meditation itself can be understood as a way of "cultivating the mind" (*citta-bhāvana*) for developing the capacity for "autonomy." According to the Buddhist doctrine of (inter)dependent-origination, however, autonomy is always relational autonomy. In informed consent, the patient autonomy cannot be separated from physicians, family members or communities. Buddhists are also concerned with the patient's psychological maturity to handle the language used when disclosing information about risks of medical treatment.

In his article "Taking Ownership: Authority and Voice in Autonomous Agency," Paul Benson points out that very often, autonomous preferences or values are subject to "direct normative constraints."[13] Some preferences are non-autonomous because of the content, so it is called a "strong substantive account" of autonomy. For example, a patient's position in his/her family would have a strong influence on his/her decision-making, even if consent is an exercise of autonomy. Meanwhile, Benson also discusses what he called a "weak substantive account" of autonomy, subject to some "normative content." Yet, it does not directly constrain the content of preferences or values. Compared with the strong account, the weak account recognizes the role of autonomy while acknowledging the nature of relationality and the nature of self-limitation. It is crucial to acknowledge the formation of individual reflections, the development of competencies and the capacity to bring one's reflections into action.

Similar to this view, Buddhism maintains that "I" exist is true only as a "convention." Buddhist scholar Jay L. Garfield speaks of synchronic unity rather than diachronic unity, contending that as long as autonomy is considered central to human agency, it requires a notion of "constructed self" that serves as the substratum.[14] At the moral level, to believe in the "self" as an enduring entity is, for Buddhists, predicated on "greed, desire, and attachment," ultimately leading to suffering. Also, the desire to construct "self-determination" inevitably leads to "selfish" concerns. Therefore, the "aim of Buddhism is . . . to realize selflessness, both metaphysically and ethically."[15]

While Buddhism challenges an individual-oriented approach to autonomy, it also challenges an individual-oriented approach to rights. Buddhism would accept "negative rights" as a protective means for the patient's interests and yet have problems with using the language of rights without qualification to grapple with every moral issue. In addition, Buddhism would also speak of the importance of duty along with the right talk. For example, in the case of vaccination, Buddhism will use duty rather than right to argue for it. In other words, it is not someone's right (i.e. individual's autonomy) to have or not have vaccination; instead, it is someone's duty to protect oneself and others in society through proper prevention of the infection and its respective immunization. Since vaccination concerns public health, Buddhists today will generally use vaccines to ensure their health is protected. However, according to some Buddhists, if the vaccine is derived from any life form (e.g. animal by-products, tested on animals), its use is debatable.[16] Those who reject using vaccines argue that treatments like antibiotics and vaccines that depend on animal experiments would generate bad karma that causes diseases.[17] However, I do not think that any Buddhist texts either support such kind of position. Given that Buddhism is not a religion confined to dogmas and one that emphasizes consequentialist considerations. Buddhism would be more acceptable to vaccination that concerns public health. One example to support this argument is vegetarianism. Despite that Buddhists practice vegetarianism in general, they can eat meat when there is no choice.

Some problems of implementing informed consent in China

There seem several potential barriers to informed consent in contemporary Chinese medical/clinical practice. In the Chinese medical or clinical setting, informed consent has not been well adopted although the idea is no longer novel. There are several problems in implementing informed consent: (1) Many people perceive informed consent due to a lack of trust due to the misunderstanding of the concept by physicians and patients.[18] (2) The ethical principle of patient autonomy and self-determination is viewed as "un-Chinese." (3) Paternalistic physicians and protective family members would counteract informed consent and very often try to make medical decisions to promote their patients' well-being independent of their wishes and values. As a result, we see the problems of misusing informed consent and persistence in obtaining consent. Treatment decisions for incompetent patients, the HIV and AIDS endemics, or minors (the vulnerable group) are another issue that required further consideration. As indicated in the document, vulnerable groups are especially susceptible to being unduly influenced into providing consent. They have a "compromised ability to protect their interests and provide informed consent" and, therefore, have a rightful claim to special consideration or protection.

In some situations, informed consent is simply a formality obtained without the patient's understanding of the physician's recommendations or adequate time to think and reflect on the recommendations. In terms of information disclosure, the physician sometimes prefers to release the information to the patient's family members rather than the patient. Some scholars in China argue that informed consent has failed to describe the role of family members in decision-making and may not work with a culture like Chinese where a physician–patient relationship becomes a physician–family–patient relationship. In some situations, excessive protection of a patient by the patient's family may also counteract informed consent. The family–patient relationship sometimes takes on a more decisive and influential role in making medical decisions than the physician–patient relationship.[19]

Many patients and family members in China (especially those from small towns and countryside) are more comfortable with the paternalistic model of the physician–patient relationship. It is still not uncommon for physicians to make unilateral decisions in the clinical setting. From a Buddhist perspective, the paternalistic model of the physician–patient relationship is sometimes necessary and, thus, should not be perceived as something consistently disruptive to informed consent. The Buddhist idea of "skilful means" (*upāya*) suggests that one should not be confined to a particular doctrine or principle; instead, one should look at a specific case in a specific context and decide accordingly.

In sum, informed consent is a complicated concept and may have desirable and undesirable effects on medical/clinical practice. Nevertheless, it is better to have it.

Notes

1 *The Nuremberg Code* says: "The voluntary consent of the human subject is absolutely essential. This means that the person involved should have legal capacity to give consent; should be so situated as to be able to exercise free power of choice, without the intervention of any element of force, fraud, deceit, duress, over-reaching, or other ulterior form of constraint or coercion; and should have sufficient knowledge and comprehension of the elements of the subject matter involved as to enable him to make an understanding and enlightened decision." Likewise, *the Declaration of Helsinki* says, "In any research on human beings,

each potential subject must be adequately informed of the aims, methods, anticipated benefits and potential hazards of the study and the discomfort it may entail. He or she should be informed that he or she is at liberty to abstain from participation in the study and that he or she is free to withdraw his or her consent to participate at any time. The physician should then obtain the subject's freely-given *informed consent*, preferably in writing.
2 Informed consent is originally a legal doctrine and was introduced into clinical medicine in the United States in the mid-1950s. Social movements regarding the rights of vulnerable groups such as minorities, women, consumers, and prisoners stimulated patients' awareness of their right to information and self-determination in clinical settings.
3 Tom L. Beauchamp and James F. Childress, *Principles of Biomedical Ethics* (Oxford: Oxford University Press, 1994), 121.
4 *Ibid.*, 157.
5 *Ibid.*, 143.
6 See UDBHR, Article 2(h).
7 Craig Ihara, "Why There Are No Rights in Buddhism: A Reply to Damien Keown," in *Buddhism and Human Rights*, ed. Damien Keown, et al. (Richmond: Curzon Press, 1998), 51.
8 People who argue for personal autonomy focus on the idea of autonomous agents whose preferences and desires are genuinely their own—as those who critically reflect in the "appropriate" way to evaluate their preferences, motives, and desires. For detailed argument, see *Autonomy and the Challenges of Liberalism*, ed. Joel Anderson and John Christman (Cambridge: Cambridge University Press, 2005).
9 Christmas Humphreys, *The Wisdom of Buddhism* (London and New York: Routledge, 1995), 79–80.
10 The idea of "impermanence" (*anitya*, Chin. *wuchang*) which refers to the conditioned phenomena arising and passing away is part of "three basic facts of existence" in early Buddhist teaching.
11 Matthew MacKenzie, "Self-Awareness without a Self: Buddhism and the Reflexivity of Awareness," *Asian Philosophy* 18, no. 3 (2008): 256.
12 Rupert Gethin, *The Foundations of Buddhism* (Oxford: Oxford University Press, 1998), 138.
13 Paul Benson, "Taking Ownership: Authority and Voice in Autonomous Agency," in *Autonomy and the Challenges of Liberalism*, ed. Joel Anderson and John Christman (Cambridge: Cambridge University Press, 2005), 133. Also see Benson, "Free Agency and Self-Worth," *Journal of Philosophy* 91, no. 12 (1994): 650–668.
14 Jay L. Garfield, *Engaging Buddhism* (Oxford: Oxford University Press, 2015), 99–100.
15 Rupert Gethin, *The Foundations of Buddhism* (Oxford: Oxford University Press, 1998), 147.
16 In fact, in some poor Buddhist countries like Cambodia and Laos, getting the vaccine is a luxury. In an area with a high degree of getting diseases, people (religious or not) do not say no to anything that might improve their odds of survival.
17 Francis Story, *Dimensions of Buddhist Thought: Collected Essays* (Sri Lanka: Buddhist Publication Society, 2012), 93.

18 Many Chinese physicians and patients do not know why and how informed consent was developed in the US (due to a series of court judgments).
19 For this argument, see Guobin Cheng, "Ethical Implication of Informed Consent:—A Case Study of 'Family Decisions' in Contemporary China," *International Journal of Chinese and Comparative Philosophy of Medicine* 15, no. 2 (2017): 21–41.

6 A Confucian view of informed consent in biomedical practice

Ruiping Fan

Introduction

To explore a Confucian view of informed consent in biomedical practice, one will first need to understand the general moral nature of Confucian tradition. Confucian tradition is not utilitarian. Neither is it grounded in a concept of individual liberty or rights. Instead, the Confucian tradition carries with it a virtue-based and virtue-oriented moral system. It takes the concept of virtue (*de*), rather than the concept of individual rights, liberty or equality, as the foundation of morality.[1] In other words, Confucianism would link human dignity with virtue, not with individual rights, liberty or equality.[2] The ultimate dignity or nobility (*gui*) of human life does not lie in enjoying rights but pursuing virtue. In short, virtue is a stable moral character by which individuals can do the right thing at the right time in the right way. Basic Confucian virtues include *ren* (humanity), *yi* (appropriateness), *li* (propriety), *zhi* (wisdom), *xin* (fidelity), *xiao* (filial piety), *he* (harmony) and so forth.

Nevertheless, human virtue is not the only intrinsic value that Confucianism pursues. Instead, Confucian tradition sees a comprehensive good human life, as it is implicit in the Confucian concept of *zhishan* (the highest good), to be a complete moral ideal at which individuals, families and governments all aim and ought to aim through personal activities and governance measures. Achieving a comprehensive good human life is comparatively similar to achieving Eudaimonia, or human flourishing, in the Greek Aristotelian sense. Importantly, pursuing the *zhishan* of human life in a properly developed Confucian tradition requires not only honouring human dignity by individuals through their exercise of the virtues but also protecting legitimate individual interests by the government. The latter can be done only through safeguarding a list of individual rights, basic liberties and equality in the state.

DOI: 10.4324/9781003213215-9

Although one may still be a virtuous, dignified person even when one's legitimate interests are violated or damaged, the state ought to protect one's legitimate interests so that one may live a comprehensively good life. This is to say, to pursue the complete ideal of human flourishing, Confucian tradition should develop a Confucian conception of human rights that has not been proposed in the tradition in the past. This conception, as well as a list of fundamental human rights covered in it, can be derived from the moral requirements of the basic Confucian virtues, such as *ren* (humanity) and *yi* (appropriateness), of which there is still general acceptance in contemporary Confucian-influenced societies.[3] However, this conception must differ from a full-brown liberal conception of human rights that imposes excessive individualistic values on other non-liberal traditions.[4] Briefly put, from a Confucian perspective, individual interest is legitimate only if it does not gravely conflict with the requirement of any basic Confucian virtue. Confucian society may tolerate certain illegitimate interests (in the sense that they may not be prohibited or punished by law) due to suitable ethical or societal concerns. However, it should not establish them (such as prostitution or gambling) as human rights or fundamental liberties. In this sense, a Confucian conception of rights will inevitably be a virtue-based conception.

Contemporary Confucian people may accept the following minimalistic list of basic rights and liberties that John Rawls has come up with for international practices in his late work. "Among the human rights are the right to life (to the means of subsistence and security); to liberty (to freedom from slavery, serfdom, and forced occupation, and to a sufficient measure of liberty of conscience to ensure freedom of religion and thought); and to formal equality as expressed by the rules of natural justice (that is, that similar cases be treated similarly)."[5] These rights and liberties can be worked out on the basis of the rationale of the Confucian *zhishan* and the virtues. They are implicit, if not explicit, in the fundamental requirements of the basic Confucian virtues regarding how individuals should treat each other and how their governments should treat them.[6] These rights should be developed and emphasized to protect legitimate individual interests in Confucian-influenced societies.

Finally, a right to informed consent for patients, subjects and their families in biomedical contexts can be worked out of the general basic right to liberty for the good human life in the Confucian tradition. Given its concern with human flourishing and virtue cultivation, Confucian tradition must accept and safeguard this right for biomedical practice. In short, although the concept of rights, in general, and a right to informed consent, in particular, were not initiated in the tradition in the past, it is only logical and reasonable for contemporary Confucianism to develop and promote such a conceptual mechanism to guide biomedical practice in Confucian society.

Informed consent in Confucian medical practice

As a virtue-based and virtue-oriented enterprise, Confucian medical ethics has traditionally accentuated the physician's virtues and obligations rather than the patient's autonomy or rights. Indeed, Confucian medicine has not had a strong tradition of practising informed consent in the past.

Specifically, Confucianism sees medicine as "the art of *ren*" (*renshu*), in contrast to politics which is seen as "the governance of *ren*" (*renzheng*). *Ren* (humanity) is the primary and complete virtue of Confucian tradition. These slogans indicate that both medicine and politics are taken to be the virtuous causes of humanity, but politics is more important than medicine. This is, perhaps, because politics can generally be used to benefit more people than medicine in most situations. Indeed, in the Confucian tradition, medicine has been termed "the little *dao*" (*xiaodao*), whereas politics "the great *dao*" (*dadao*).[7] Meanwhile, both traditional Confucian politics and medicine have a meritocratic and paternalistic tendency: only virtuous persons should become politicians or physicians, and they should make decisions to promote people's welfare in light of their professional knowledge and judgements. In medicine, Confucian physician ethics has been similar to the Hippocratic Oath ethics in terms of medical professional obligations. It is the health and well-being of the patient that constitute the end of the art of medicine. But, the judgement of such health and well-being lies in the hands of the physician. Throughout the history of Chinese medicine, the physician's virtue and obligation in performing the art of *ren* in assisting patients and their families have always been emphasized. It has never been required of the physician to provide sufficient information to patients or their families. In reality, Chinese physicians must have normally gained consent, either explicitly or implicitly, from their patients or families before administering medical treatment.[8] Nevertheless, it is also clear that obtaining such consent before conducting treatment has never been formally stipulated in the tradition.

However, such a lack of an explicit requirement of informed consent from the patient has been mixed with another prominent feature of Confucian medical ethics: shared family decision-making for the medical matters of the patient. It is important not to lose sight of this remarkable Confucian familist feature in biomedical practice.

As is well known, the Chinese character *ren* (as Confucian complete virtue) is etymologically made up of the element "person" and the number "two," meaning that one cannot become a virtuous (authentic) human being simply by oneself. By extension, it means that the *dao* (way) of the good life consists in forming appropriate human relationships in leading one's life. Confucius (551–479 BCE) states that *ren* primarily requires loving humans

(*Analects* 12: 12).[9] One must begin the practice of love from one's family and extend it to other people. So the principle of love under the Confucian virtue of *ren* is not only universal (namely, one should love all human beings) but also differentiated and non-egalitarian (namely, one should love one's family members more than other people; so love is relevant to relations in ordinary situations). It is the family, rather than separate individuals, that constitutes the ultimately autonomous unit of decision-making from the rest of society. As Confucian people understand the unity of the family as modelling after the primordial unity of *yin* and *yang*, two basic types of *qi* (as the fundamental elements of the universe), living united and harmonious family lives is precisely for Confucian people to follow the Dao of Heaven.

The family plays a crucial role in taking care of the sick and making shared medical decisions for them in Confucian society. The patient is always taken to be a patient in the family, and a family member's illness is taken to be the issue of the whole family. The family must undertake special fiduciary obligations to care for the ill member. The Chinese physician typically discusses the diagnosis, prognosis and treatment of a severely ill patient with his or her family members. Patients themselves should be left to relax and rest, not to be bothered by making serious communication with physicians. They are usually more than willing to be represented by their family members for their medical arrangements. The family has the final authority to accept or refuse the physician's prescription for the patient. This familist pattern of medical decision-making is appreciated as removing unnecessary burdens from the patient in the medical process, such as listening to and discussing with the physician, unless the patient strongly wants to engage in the process. Confucian people take it for granted that families ought to undertake such burdens for their ill family members. If the family believes that the information of a fatal diagnosis or prognosis will harm the patient and discount the efficacy of treatment, they would ask the physician to hide the truth from the patient, and the physician would generally follow the request. Physicians generally take it unsympathetic (and unvirtuous) if they directly disclose such harsh information to the patient without obtaining the consent of the family in the first place. Instead of seeking a signature for surgery directly from the patient, Chinese physicians usually obtain a signature from a family representative on behalf of the whole family, including the patient. In short, in the Confucian tradition, the family is responsible for every family member's healthcare, financially, emotionally and morally.

Contemporary Confucianism must explicitly reject physician paternalism (namely, the physician should make medical decisions for the patient according to the physician's judgement of the patient's well-being) because it violates the patient's right to informed consent that Confucianism should integrate. As discussed in the first section, individual rights, as a moral and legal mechanism, are necessary to protect legitimate individual interests essential for living a comprehensive good human life, even if they are not essential for living a virtuous human life. For the sake of patients' legitimate interests, physicians must be required to provide relevant medical information to patients and their families. It should be the patients and their families, rather than physicians, that have the final authority to decide about medical care issues for the patients.

On the other hand, Confucian medical familism (in the sense that the entire family, the patient included, rather than a single patient him- or herself, should be the final authority to make healthcare decisions) should be maintained in contemporary society with specific qualifications.[10] First, contemporary patients should be encouraged to engage in deliberations for their medical care decisions with their family members, and they should not leave all medical issues only to their family members as they did in the past. When patients are very passive in the medical process, it not only imposes unbearably heavy burdens on their family members to make decisions on their behalf but also not contributive to making the best possible decisions for their medical interests. However, for medical treatment, patients should not be granted an exclusive right to refuse medical treatment regardless of their families' views in the Confucian tradition. If the patient's immediate family members unanimously hold that the patient's refusal of medical treatment is violating the patient's medical best interests, and the physician supports this view, then the patient's refusal should be overridden. On the other hand, for non-therapeutic medical experiments, the family does not have a right to require any family member to participate in a medical trial although the family can affirm or deny a member's consent to become a research subject. This asymmetrical requirement is necessary for protecting the vital interests of family members in considering the likely benefits and risks of a medical experiment on the patient.[11] For Confucians, the family veto power in such circumstances is necessary to protect the patient's legitimate medical interests. Finally, although the physician can generally follow a family's decision to hide the truth from the patient to protect the patient, the physician must communicate directly with the patient and tell the patient the truth if the physician finds that either of the two following conditions has not been met. First, there is evidence of manifest mutual concern of the family members for the patient. Second, the family's wishes are not egregiously in discord with the physician's professional judgement regarding the medical best interests of the patient.[12]

With these qualifications and specifications, the practice of a Confucian familist approach to informed consent should not be taken to be depriving the right to self-determination of the patient. Instead, it is undertaking the fiduciary obligation of the family to care for an ill family member and seek a comprehensive good life for the patient. Accordingly, although contemporary Confucian people must reject medical paternalism, they do not have to shift to an individualist approach to informed consent. "This shift has often taken place through the influence of Western advocates, who falsely portray their own morality as a set of universal ethical principles, regardless of cultural context."[13] The proper Confucian medical context should be one in which the patient is virtuously taken care of.

Does this Confucian familist approach to informed consent violate the principle of autonomy? The answer depends on which principle of autonomy is referred to.[14] It certainly conflicts with the liberal individualist principle of autonomy because this principle requires that one always act on one's reasons or wishes to make decisions and never submit to another authority without losing autonomy. However, as Beauchamp and Childress point out, "no fundamental inconsistency exists between autonomy and authority if individuals exercise their autonomy in choosing to accept an institution, tradition, or community that they view as a legitimate source of direction."[15] People in the Confucian tradition have autonomously accepted the family's authority (in which the patient is included as a member) for determining medical issues for family members. It is "autonomous" because this process of acceptance can arguably be understood to be intentional, with understanding, and without external controlling influences, to meet the three-condition standard of autonomy that has been constructed by Beauchamp and Childress.[16] From this Confucian familist approach to informed consent, individual autonomy and family autonomy can converge into a mutually-cared process of deliberation in which family members communicate with each other and with the physician to make medical decisions for the patient to accomplish the best medical interests of the patient. Burden is on those individuals who do not accept this Confucian familist approach to informed consent in Confucian society to inform their physicians about their individualist preferences in the first place in order to to receive different treatment.

Concluding remarks

In short, the Confucian account of informed consent for biomedical practice is not an individualist account, in which the individual is appreciated as possessing sole or exclusive decisional authority in biomedical matters independently of one's family. Instead, the Confucian approach to informed consent is virtue-based and family-oriented. It accentuates the naturalness, usefulness and normalness of the engagement of family members in a patient's biomedical decision-making, thus acknowledging a shared decisional authority granted by both the patient and the family.[17] If the patient and the immediate family members hold disagreement regarding biomedical issues, they need to work out a solution through reasonable discussion in light of the moral requirements of the virtues. Sometimes, the physician may play a crucial role in providing advice and standing on the patient's or the family's side to tip the scale.[18] As to a question regarding how this familist model of informed consent would imply for those patients who have no families, it should be left to another chance to discuss.

Notes

1 Ruiping Fan, *Reconstructionist Confucianism: Rethinking Morality after the West* (Dordrecht: Springer, 2010).
2 Joseph Chan, *Confucian Perfectionism* (Princeton: Princeton University Press, 2014).
3 Fan, *Reconstructionist Confucianism*.
4 Ruiping Fan and Wenqing Zhao, "Developing Confucian Virtue-Based Rights: A Response to Jonathan Chan's Confucian Critique of the Universal Declaration on Bioethics and Human Rights," in *Religious Perspectives on Bioethics and Human Rights*, ed. Joseph Tham, Kai Man Kwan, and Alberto Garcia (Dordrecht: Springer, 2017), 115–118.
5 John Rawls, *Law of Peoples* (Cambridge: Harvard University Press, 1999), 65.
6 From a Confucian moral perspective, some more rights, such as elderly parents' right to receive their adult children's care, may need to be supplemented to this minimal list of human rights for Confucian-influenced societies. However, this paper will not address this issue due to the limit of space.
7 As a Confucian politician, Fan Zhongyan (989–1052) has famously stated: "if one cannot become a good premier, one should become a good physician." His reason is as follows: "If one can become a good premier and implement the *dao* of a sage king, one will be able to benefit everyone under-the-Heaven, both nobles and ordinary men. However, if one is not able to become a good premier, then nothing is better than becoming a good physician to practice the art of saving humans and benefiting things. Only a good physician, although staying below, is able to offer help to both his superiors and subordinates. To his superiors he can cure the ailments of his parents and emperor, to his subordinates he can rescue them from their maladies, and to himself he can preserve his life and pursue longevity." For details, see Ruiping Fan, "The Discourses of Confucian Medical Ethics," in *The Cambridge World History of Medical Ethics*, ed. Robert Baker and Laurence McCullough (Cambridge: Cambridge University Press, 2009), 195–201.
8 As I will show subsequently, medical familism has been strong in Confucian tradition and set up the familist feature of informing family members rather than the patient in Chinese medicine. For example, a famous Han dynasty physician, Chun Yuyi (ca. 215–150 BCE), put it clearly: diagnosis of any severe disease should not be disclosed to the patient, but it should be told only to the family. For details, see Ruiping Fan and Benfu Li, "Truth Telling in Medicine: The Confucian View," *Journal of Medicine and Philosophy* 29, no. 2 (2004): 179–193.
9 Mencius (372–289 BEC), following Confucius, gives a further account of *ren* that subsequent Confucian scholars have accepted: the root of *ren* lies in the

human heart that cannot bear the suffering of the other (*Mencius* 2A: 6). Every human heart (*xin*) has this capacity of sympathy because it has been endowed by Heaven (*tian*) with refined *qi*, fundamental elements of the universe. This capacity of sympathy forms the potentials of the virtues for one to develop in the Confucian tradition. So a human heart naturally holds sympathetic reactions to the *qi* of other hearts. For Mencius, one must nourish and cultivate one's vast, flowing *qi* to become virtuous (*Mencius* 2A: 2).

10 In contemporary Confucian-influenced societies, the family typically includes a patient's immediate family members, such as spouses, children, and biological parents. Sometimes the patient's siblings are also included.
11 Rui Deng, "The Informed Consent of Human Medical Research in Mainland China: A Family-Based Binary Decision Model," in *Family Based Informed Consent: East Asian and American Perspectives*, ed. Ruiping Fan (Dordrecht: Springer, 2015), 201–218.
12 Fan and Li, "Truth Telling in Medicine: The Confucian View."
13 Lin Bian, "Medical Individualism or Medical Familism? A Critical Analysis of China's New Guidelines for Informed Consent: The Basic Norms of the Documentation of the Medical Record," *Journal of Medicine and Philosophy* 40, no. 4 (2015): 371–386 at 372.
14 Ruiping Fan, "Self-Determination vs. Family-Determination: Two Incommensurable Principles of Autonomy," *Bioethics* 11, no. 3–4 (1997): 309–322.
15 Tom Beauchamp and James Childress, *Principles of Biomedical Ethics*, 7th ed. (Oxford: Oxford University Press, 2013), 105.
16 *Ibid.*, 104.
17 Ruiping Fan, "Informed Consent: Why Family-Oriented?," in *Family Based Informed Consent: East Asian and American Perspectives*, ed. Ruiping Fan (Dordrecht: Springer, 2015), 3–23.
18 Fan and Li, "Truth Telling in Medicine: The Confucian View."

7 Hindu norms on human experimentation

Parsing classical texts

John Lunstroth

Introduction

The contemporary requirement that subjects of human experimentation give their informed or free consent to being an experimental subject was first enunciated as a universal norm in the military tribunals after World War Two. The United States brought charges against Karl Brandt, M.D. and 22 others alleging they had committed war crimes by overseeing the Holocaust. In what was to become the Nuremberg Code, Judges Beals, Sebring and Crawford ruled that

> All agree, however, that certain basic principles must be observed in order to satisfy moral, ethical, and legal concepts:
>
> 1. The voluntary consent of the human subject is essential . . . .[1]

The Nuremberg Code, although pronounced as self-evident norms that already existed in the natural legal order, was not only not understood to be principles of international law, it was almost immediately widely seen as far too stringent to be of any use.[2] That being said, in 1966, after 18 years of negotiation, the United Nations put up for signature the two covenants that would define the international human rights regime, the International Covenant on Civil and Political Rights (ICCPR) and the International Covenant on Economic, Social and Cultural Rights.[3] Article 7 of the ICCPR states, in its entirety, simply that

> No one shall be subjected to torture or to cruel, inhuman or degrading treatment or punishment. In particular, no one shall be subjected without his free consent to medical or scientific experimentation.[4]

In 1976, the ICCPR came into force, and within a few years was understood to enunciate universal principles of international law.[5] That meant that not

DOI: 10.4324/9781003213215-10

only were signatories bound by the ICCPR, including India, but even non-signatory states were by application of the principle of universality.[6]

Bioethicists in the global environment seek to understand whether norms such as this can be justified in, or supported by, the various religious traditions since the international human rights regime can be seen as secular, Eurocentric and echoing colonial sentiments.[7] In comparing religions as sources of relevant norms, Hinduism is often queried. Although this query appears on its face to make sense, scholars of subcontinent traditions generally agree that Hinduism is not a religion in the sense of having either a central doctrine or a central authority.[8] It has neither. Prior to colonial influences, the word referred to the peoples of the subcontinent.[9] Colonial institutions and authorities, for various political and economic reasons, used their notions of religion to order those peoples, in the process creating religion as a form of self-identity with political features in the late eighteenth and nineteenth centuries.[10] Hinduism came to be distinguished in the colonial context, more or less, from [the religion of] Islam. One of the distinguishing features of this new colonial Hinduism was its foundation in Vedic and related ancient or classical Sanskrit texts.[11]

I argue later that because bioethics is a function of the political order, only one class of ancient texts, those addressing political order/theory, can be potential justifications of or support for norms regarding bioethics. The central text of this textual tradition is Kautilya's *Arthasastra*.[12] This text purports to give a king comprehensive advice about all aspects of administering a kingdom. It is decidedly secular, treating those we might identify as the religious, including monks and renunciates, at best as potential spies and operatives, or treating religiosity as a good cover for them. Religion, to the extent it is recognized in the text, is entirely instrumentalized for the secular order. However, there is a textual basis for the kingdom's interest in maintaining public health, and doctors of both men and horses are also recognized as having a special status.

There are two ways the original query can be addressed in this context. One, the *Arthasastra* can be projected onto the Constitution of India. Like the ideal kingdom described in the *Arthasastra*, India is established by its constitution as a secular state. In that analysis, being a citizen of India would be read as the central case of what it means to be a Hindu,[13] and the Constitution would be read as the fundamental source of bioethical norms. That would focus the query, for example, on the fundamental rights defined in the Constitution, including the rights of equality (Arts 14), freedom of speech (Art 19) and freedom of religion (Art 25) and the obligations of the state for the improvement of public health (Art 47). This would require complex analysis and comparison of the *Arthasastra* and the Indian state, an important project but beyond the remit of this paper. Two, the analysis could more simply examine whether the *Arthasastra* has any norms that could directly be applied to issues related to human experimentation. I will take this approach.

India presents complexity when considering human experimentation and consent. It is in the process of modernizing and has one foot in the past and one in the future. The upper strata of the middle class and above are more heavily influenced by global trends, while the rest of society lives in conditions more continuous with the less affluent India of the 1970s and earlier. The global trend would suggest that norms of autonomy would dictate individual consent is central to medical or scientific interventions of any kind.[14] On the other hand, large and powerful pharmaceutical companies seek to utilize entire populations without significant regard for individual consent.[15] So, for the more affluent, consent in human experimentation presents the same kind of problem it does in the West, but the less affluent subjects of human experimentation face a different set of problems because those citizens rely more heavily on the state for protection from the private sector.

Seeking bioethical norms in the classical Sanskrit texts

The classical Sanskrit literature of India describes several ways to categorize human existence.[16] There are four stages (Skt. *chaturashramas*) that are loosely age-based: *brahmacharya* (student), *grihastha* (householder), *vanaprastha* (retired) and *sannyasa* (renunciation). There are four goals of the human life (*puruṣartha*): *artha* (socio-economic position); *kama* (fulfilling desired); *dharma* (being virtuous) and *moksha* (liberation). There are four classes (*varṇas*) of human beings: *brahmins* (priests); *Kshatriyas* (rulers); *vaishyas* (merchants) and *Shudras* (labourers).

The canonical Sanskrit texts that can be evaluated as potential sources of bioethical norms are clearly divided into four categories, one for each of the four goals of human life.[17] This makes sense as the different stages/purposes of life are defined by different normative systems or *dharmas*.

First, consider the four stages of life. The first stage, *brahmacharya* (student), prepares one for the following *grihastha* (householder) stage. Once that stage is finished, one enters the *vanaprastha* (retired) stage in which one prepares for the final *sannyasa* (renunciate) stage. Thus, there are two main ways of being in human life. One prepares for and then exists as a householder, and then one prepares for and becomes a renunciate.

Each of these major ways of being (i.e. stages of life) is characterized by certain purposes. The householder is concerned with material and physical well-being, with marriage, children and career (*artha* and *kama*) and with leading a righteous law-abiding life (*dharma*). For this, there are rules contained in the canonical texts known as *sutras* and *shastras*. Accordingly, there are texts collected under the rubric of *kama*,[18] under the rubric of *artha*[19] and under the rubric of *dharma*.[20] Under the *dharma* of being a householder also fall some of the much earlier *Vedic Samhitas*, especially the *Rigveda*, *Yajurveda* and *Samaveda*. These texts cover reciting hymns (*Rigveda*), performing sacrifices (*Yajurveda*) and chanting songs (*Samaveda*), that is, recitations, ceremonies and rituals for many aspects of day-to-day life that focus on being a good householder and are overseen by *Vedic* (*Brahmin*) priests. The *Vedic* ordering of society fostered a complex legacy of both compassion and tolerance for and towards the other, a sense of fundamental identity with the other, as well as intense inequities, such as the caste system. These legacies were formative in all of the Subcontinent traditions and probably reflected the norms of communal life that formed the earliest communities. The legacies of the *Vedic* order were influential in the Jain, Buddhist, Moslem and other traditions although in Jainism and Buddhism, there were canonical rejections of some of the inequities (such as the caste system).

The main purpose of renunciation, of *moksha* (liberation), is contained in a great wealth of other canonical texts, starting with the final layers of the *Vedas* known as the *Upanishads*.[21] The *Upanishads* are grouped with two other texts, the *Brahma Sutras*[22] and *Bhagavad Gita*,[23] and are said to make up the teachings of *Vedanta*, or the completion or fulfilment of the *Vedas*.[24] These texts focus on the state of *moksha*. *Moksha* is obtained or attained after long years spent in seclusion meditating. Moving towards *moksha* after the purposes of life as a householder have been fulfilled, which is the natural progression of a fully lived life, first means separating from the family. This increasing separation is the *vanaprastha* stage that precedes life as a *sannyasin* or renunciate that has attained *moksha*. Although connected to a human body, the sannyasin experiences his/her self (i.e. *atman*, pure consciousness) as completely free, and for the more advanced experiences, their *atman* as being one with *Brahman* (the source of consciousness). This state of being is discussed using abstract concepts, including *dharma*, *karma*, *samsara*, *guru*, *atman* and *Brahman*. A central tenet is that direct knowledge (*samadhi*) of these abstract concepts is possible through *sadhana* (meditation).

The *moksha* state of being is profoundly disconnected from and finds no meaning in the political order or any aspect of the *brahmacharya*, *grihastha* or *vanaprastha* stages of life. These beings are even said to exist without ethics or morals, in the sense that there is no need for them to consider what is right since everything they do is in accord with nature and the true Self and cannot be unethical. They are not ethical beings, as they are completely liberated. It is a very refined, rarified and subtle state of being. These beings live not according to *artha–kama–dharma* but according to *moksha dharma*.[25] The perfect man is no longer bound by humankind's ethics, laws or order (*dharma*).[26] In Aristotle's formulation in the Politics, they would be gods since they are no longer political animals.[27]

To summarize, there is a difference between life as a householder (*grihastha*) and life as a renunciate (*sannyasa*). These are two centres of gravity, each with its own *dharma*. The renunciate lives apart from society at large and is directly familiar with the abstract concepts that order existence. The householder is embedded in the political/economic order and is not expected to have direct knowledge of the abstract concepts.

The householder could be said to be religious to the extent he follows the ritual norms laid down in the Vedas, but Hinduism cannot be restricted to that set of norms. Since Jainism, Buddhism and Sikhism are all Hindu, and they reject Vedic norms, then whatever a Hindu is, he is not necessarily in the Vedic spirit. The presence of the entirely secular political theory of the *Arthasastra* complicates matters even more. If Hinduism is linked to the Vedic and subsequent classical Sanskrit tradition, including Jainism, Buddhism and secularism, there is no common thing that can be identified as Hindu religion.

Because ethics is a property of political/legal order, I argue that in Hinduism, bioethics is proper for the householder, but not the renunciate and that the abstract concepts (i.e. *karma* and *atman*) are inapt in bioethical analyses.[28] Therefore, we would search the *kama*, *artha* and *dharma* texts for norms that could apply to today's bioethical problems. Of these textual traditions, only one concerns itself with systematic theories of political/legal order (i.e. *dharma*), represented best by the *Arthasastra* of *Kautilya*.[29] It presents a thoroughly secular, intensely practical manual for a king, generalized to an ideal kingdom. In that kingdom, the king freely uses all of the institutions surrounding *moksha dharma* for political purposes. There is no concern for the concepts of *karma*, *atman*, *Brahman*, *moksha*, etc., except that the king's spies and operatives can pretend to be of this class of people to infiltrate groups and otherwise work for the maintenance of political and economic order. The king is concerned with his own pleasure and the kingdom's political and economic stability. Much of the book is concerned with maintaining order at the borders of the kingdom, with war and the maintenance of order in far-flung regions. There is a fairly well-developed idea of public order that includes the maintenance of public health, and doctors are recognized as an important part of society, to the extent they can be used as spies at times, and spies can pretend to be doctors for their covert purposes.

Contemporary consent issues in human experimentation

There are three central issues raised by human experimentation today. The first centres on the requirement for human subjects to give consent to being experimented upon. A second recognizes that the central ethical calculus of human experimentation is sacrifice. The third explores ethical issues regarding the financial consequences of human experimentation.

Consent

Informed, free or voluntary consent is universally recognized as a right of human subjects. The right is based on fundamental notions of autonomy, of the right to self-direct. It is much discussed and, at this point, somewhat unremarkable as an individual right. However, human experiments are not done on individuals because the goal of a human experiment is a statistical picture of the experimental intervention. In developing the statistical picture, the individuality of the subject cannot be considered, only the clinical effects of the intervention. The individual subject disappears into the statistical cohort. This means that a key ethical entity is the cohort of experimental subjects, not any of them individually. In this context, the two ultimate purposes of human experimentation, advances in knowledge and profits, give rise to the two other central ethical problems.

Sacrifice

It is well understood that human experimentation for the development of drugs, devices and treatments is grounded in the civil need for sacrifice.[30] Sacrifice is understood to be for both the community and science.[31] The Belmont Report, one of the foundational ethical documents in the area of human experimentation, makes this clear regarding science in its discussion of the ethical principle of beneficence:

> In the case of scientific research in general, members of the larger society are obliged to recognize the longer term benefits and risks that may result from the improvement of knowledge and from the development of novel medical, psychotherapeutic, and social procedures.[32]

Pope Pius XII, at the very beginning of the radical increase in the authority of science and the production of drugs, in reflecting on the Nuremberg Medical Case, recognizes that the community has a claim on the individual to participate in experimentation for the benefit of the individual, the community and science. However, it must be subject to proper understanding and limits.[33] Not only must the experiments be serious, honest and promote the practice of medicine, but the state must also approve them. Private approval is ethically unacceptable because of the nature of the community. The community is not a whole made up of parts; rather, each element of the state participates fully in the essence of the state. If the state permitted the private sector to conduct research willy-nilly, it would be abrogating its responsibility to protect the individual.

> It must be noted that, in his personal being, man is not finally ordered to usefulness to society. On the contrary, the community exists for man.[34]

However, there is yet another theory of Lockean implicit consent, in which a state made up of individuals has agreed to a certain kind of unity or governance. Locke developed the idea of tacit or implied consent to justify acts of the government, among other things, those for the benefit of the citizenry.[35] Thus, the argument can be made that the polity, acting through its representative government, has approved the willing sacrifice of individuals for scientific knowledge for the good of the community and the individual. Pope Pius XII argues that this is the kind of sacrifice that is misguided.

Profits

The central case of human experimentation is as follows. Researchers for pharmaceutical companies develop chemical compounds that could be used to treat diseases. These compounds begin life as trade secrets, and at some point, if they have promise, they are patented. A patent is a legal monopoly on the compound. Having a patent is not enough to be able to market a compound, however. Before a compound can be marketed, the pharmaceutical company must prove, according to certain standards, to the drug regulatory agencies that the compound is relatively safe if used a certain way and relatively effective for the condition being treated. If the proof is sufficient, the agency may permit the company to market the compound for the intended use. If the agency approves the compound for marketing, it requires the company to label the compound to inform doctors and patients of the identity of the disease it treats and the nature, risks and benefits of the compound. Once labelled, the compound has legal status as a drug. The exclusive approval to market the drug combined with the patent gives the pharmaceutical company complete control over the market for the drug for the patent period.

Although the costs of developing a drug are unknown, closely guarded trade secrets, the drug companies allege they are astronomical. One study reported that the average cost is $2.7 billion.[36] A more nuanced and transparent study reported that the median cost of bringing a single cancer drug to market is $648 million, and the median revenue is $1.7 billion.[37] Some drugs have star status, blockbuster drugs. These generate at least $1 billion a year for the owner. Although very few drugs become blockbusters, their potential drives the industry. Total worldwide pharmaceutical sector revenues were more than $1.1 trillion in 2017, making it in the top 2 or 3 economic sectors globally.[38] Profit margins are in the 25%–30% range, making total global profits in the pharmaceutical sector over $250 billion.

> More than any other industry, the pharmaceutical sector is highly dependent on its research and development segment. . . . Because of the steady loss of patent protection, the invention of new drugs is of vital importance for the pharmaceutical industry. Revenue losses due to patent expiry often are very significant.[39]

The foregoing detail is warranted to understand the importance of two kinds of people or roles in the pharmaceutical industry, physicians and subjects, both somewhat invisible in the earlier description.

Physicians are required because they are the gatekeepers to the drugs through their prescription writing authority. Sales of prescription drugs "by far" account for most industry revenues.[40] Industry advertises directly either to physicians or to consumers with the directive to ask their physician for the drug. In 2016, pharmaceutical advertising in the United States alone was ~$30 billion, about $20 billion to physicians and $9 billion to consumers.[41] On gross revenues in the United States of about $446 billion (2016)[42] that is about 7%.

The human experimental subject is the other role of paramount importance. Without subjects, no drug could ever enter the market. Subjects are essential in developing knowledge of safety and efficacy, the necessary ingredient in drug[43] research and development (R&D). In 2016, industry spent $60 billion on R&D, or about 14% of revenues.[44]

Although doctors get some financial benefit from the money spent by industry to woo them,[45] subjects get virtually none. It is this fact, I want to use as the entry point into using sacrifice as an ethical model to understand human experimentation. Subjects can be looked at from two perspectives. On the one hand, they are considered individuals, human beings with dignity, who volunteer to be experimented on. On the other hand, the individuality of the subject is not relevant, rather the value/data from the individual is merged with that from other subjects to become the statistical whole, and statistical knowledge of the cohort is what has value. The ethical relationship between the pharmaceutical company and the subject ends when the raw data have been taken from the subject. Statistical knowledge of the whole is a new ethical entity in the existing system that privileges the creation of private property from the experiment.

After the development of a promising compound, the pharmaceutical company must research its safety and efficacy. Knowledge of safety and efficacy must be to standards set by the regulatory industry. Since the United States is one of the most important and largest markets for drugs (45% of the global market),[46] the standards set by its regulatory agency, the U.S. Food & Drug Administration (FDA), are considered exemplary.

The FDA requires quantitative, that is, statistical, measures derived from randomized controlled trials (experiments) to evaluate safety and efficacy. Drug companies design protocols that establish the parameters of the experiments, which must be conducted on human beings. Generally, the FDA must approve experiments in which the data and statistics will be used in an application-seeking market approval. For each potential drug/disease, the FDA and company agree on the number of experimental subjects that the experiments must conduct.

Recruitment of subjects is an area fraught with ethical problems, such as payments received by treating physicians for successful referrals, the therapeutic misconception and others. However, the legal principles that transform a person with a full set of rights into a subject with no rights regarding the researchers are the operative acts establishing the possibility of the sacrifice.

When a person agrees to participate in an experiment, he or she must consent to be a participant. The consent document, by law, is supposed to fully inform the potential subject of the risks and benefits of the experimental intervention. In a standard legal transaction, the informed consent document would have the force of a contract.[47] A contract would, typically, provide a quid quo pro for things given or received, and, finally, a contract would be the basis for a cause of action in the event there were damages to person or things caused by one of the parties to the contract.[48] In fact, the informed consent document does none of these things. It is not construed by courts to be a contract;[49] it provides, if anything, for only a nominal payment for participation,[50] and it provides no cause of action in the event of an injury.[51]

The sacrifice can be described in the terms set forth earlier. A sacrifice is the killing or destruction of something of value to influence the future.[52] The influence on the future, on nature, occurs through the mediation of the god or other authority in charge of the future who is the intended recipient of the value. That is, the sacrificer takes value from a thing (usually a living thing) by destroying it, transforms it into something invisible and transfers it to the authority to enhance the position of the intended beneficiary of the sacrifice (which does not have to be the sacrificer).

In a scientific experiment, a human being is transformed into an experimental subject. The value of the subject is a kind of biological machine into which an intervention is introduced. Information from the subject is then used to measure the intervention. The humanity of the subject was abandoned regarding the process when the informed consent was signed. The being on which the experiment is being performed is not fully human anymore, concerning the process.

This is a sacrifice in three senses, or it could be said there are three sacrificers and two sacrifices. In one sense, individuals sacrifice themselves and their rights for one of two purposes: to help themselves or help others. In most cases, the first reason cannot be true because it results from the therapeutic misconception, in which potential subjects are mistakenly convinced the experimental treatment will benefit them.[53] The second reason is not valid because none of the research benefits will be freely available to the public except the drug if the experiment can be made successful, and then the public is charged an often obscene amount of money for the drug.[54] The only advancement of science from drug research occurs within the silos of the individual drug companies. The god is science and truth, neither of which exists in the sacrificial space, and thus the sacrifice for better health and scientific knowledge must usually fail.

In the second sense, the drug company sacrifices the individuals who "consent" to participate. The company strips value from them, aggregates and then monetizes it for itself. The god is the neoliberal economic system that awards greed, and the sacrifice usually works.

In the third sense, the U.S. government has established and maintains the legal and institutional arrangements that support the neoliberal values that encourage individuals to sacrifice themselves out of ignorance and the pharmaceutical companies to sacrifice individuals for their profits. That is, the U.S. government offers its citizens up for sacrifice by the companies. Its sacrifices fail to the extent citizens are not protected and succeed to the extent the large pharmaceutical companies reap extraordinary profits.

If the purity of the sacrificial or ritual space is considered, another set of interesting issues arise. In both cases, the sacrificial space is impure since the individual participates out of ignorance and selfishness, and the company misleads the sacrificial subjects to get them to participate. Why does the sacrifice generally fail for the individual and succeed for the company? One reason could be that the individual does not have the power to influence the gods to which his or her sacrifice is directed, truth and science. A related or underlying question must query whether the individual has a duty to look into the true nature of the sacrifice, whether it is, in fact, possible for there to be a therapeutic benefit or whether the information from the experiment would ever become part of the public domain. The negative answer to these queries is readily available on the internet, but most regular people do not have enough experience and background knowledge to know they can ask those questions, and the authority of the system keeps them in ignorance. They are taught to trust science and scientists. If the potential subject learned the truth, it would seem there would be no motivation to participate. This explains why there is a cloak of ignorance spread in the general population about the benefits and nature of human experimentation.

But the lesson from the success of the drug company is that the ignorance of the sacrificed thing is no bar to the value being conveyed to the god of the neoliberal system, who can then confer its rewards, profits to the company. This would be consistent with the sacrifice of non-human animals and inanimate things. The status of their consciousness is irrelevant to their value to the god.

Consent and sacrifice in the *Arthasastra*

Sacrifice in the Vedas

The *Arthasastra* was written in the milieu of the *Vedas*. Although it is difficult to date the Vedic texts with any accuracy, it is not unreasonable to say the core *Vedic* texts were relatively complete by about 1,500 BCE.[55] They underlay what developed into the *dharma sastric* tradition, a very legalistic system in which the dharma, or heavenly order governing day-to-day life, was controlled by the Brahmanical priestly class.[56] Sacrifice is central to the *Vedic* texts to insure dharma is maintained in the relations between the non-human and human realms. For the most part, it was controlled by the priestly class, but individuals could also perform some rituals. By the time the *Arthasastra* was written or compiled (c 50–125 CE),[57] Vedic traditions had crystallized into an oppressive system of laws and rules controlled by the priesthood that governed all aspects of householder life.[58] The legalism caused widespread counter-movements, including the formation of Jainism and Buddhism and the developments in the theory of government reflected in the Arthasastra. The political theory became secular and pluralistic and instrumentalized the Vedic legalism for political ends.

That being said, sacrifice is mentioned throughout the *Arthasastra*, and the tradition of sacrifice it principally refers to is that practised by the *Brahmin* priests based in *Vedic* texts. To understand sacrifice in the Vedas, it is necessary to be aware of their texts and layers.[59]

There are four *Vedas*: the *Rig Veda*, the *Sama Veda*, the *Yajur Veda* and the *Atharva Veda*. The *Rig Veda* contains hymns (chants, mantras) primarily to various deities; the *Sama Veda* contains excerpts from the *Rig Veda*; the *Yajur Veda* contains, in addition to *Rig Veda* hymns, sacrificial prayers or formulas and the *Atharva Veda* consists of a special class of texts dealing with spells, incantations and kingly duties as well as exalted spiritual truths.

Each Veda has two sections. The *Mantra* is the collection of hymns used in the sacrifices, and the *Brahmana* contains the accessories, rules and regulations for the sacrifices and discloses the meaning of the mantras, which otherwise might remain obscure. Vedic sacrifice was an extremely important way people communed with the gods (deities, higher powers). The sacrifices are "offerings of oblations for the propitiation of the deities."[60]

Two additional layers of the *Vedas*, developments within the *Brahmana* according to Nikhilananda, are the *Aranyakas* and the *Upanishads*. The *Aranyaka*, or "forest-treatise," was aimed at the person in the third stage of life, *vanaprastha*. This person has become a hermit and is living apart as he prepares for *moksha* (liberation) and the *sannyasin* stage. Since the sacrifices required and described in the other parts of the *Veda* are too expensive and impractical for the hermit, the *Aranyaka* "prescribes symbolic worship and describes various meditations" that are used as substitutes for the sacrifices. Worship is transformed to the mental level from the physical. The *Upanishads* are the most recent layer of the *Vedas* and describe the abstract principles that are characteristic of the liberated person. Sacrifice per se is not necessary for the sannyasin since his obligations have all been subsumed in his inner attainment or perfection.

Consent and sacrifice in the Arthasastra

The text of the Arthasastra contains many examples of rules governing day-to-day life such as litigation, family law matters, inheritance, criminal behaviour, property, boundaries, debt, slaves and labourers, commercial transactions and gambling.[61] Topic 24, Organization of Revenue Collection by the Collector, covers all the myriad ways a government raises money, including, for example, from taxes, fines, duties and it covers such topics as standardizations of weights and measures.[62]

It is clear from the text that physicians play an important role and that there is a system of drugs, pharmacies and pharmaceutical companies regulated for safety and honesty.[63] Although it is exactly the same form as it is today, there is a fundamental difference between *Ayurveda* and scientific medicine that radically changes the context and makes the notion of experiment much less likely to occur in the same way. Ayurveda is a revealed set of doctrines, like Chinese medicine and homoeopathy, and investigation of substances occurs through a process of Aristotelian *epagoge*, in which reasoning begins with first principles and, for example, the medicinal powers of substances would be described and tested under the framework of the first principles.[64] The first principles are never questioned. There would be no inductive epistemological activity in the ways understood in a contemporary drug investigation.

I describe the polity because it is only possible to infer the capacity of individuals to consent in the sense of an individual consenting to be experimented on. Presumably, in this hierarchical society, those with less status have correlatively less capacity to consent, whereas high-status persons would have greater capacity. Would the king require such experiments for public health purposes, he could order people to participate. How he would determine who was chosen is not clear.

However, because sacrifices are such a big part of day-to-day life, and people pay priests and others for the materials and expertise to make sacrifices, sacrifice is a regulated economic and civil activity. We can identify at least one norm in the *Arthasastra* that is more directly applicable to contemporary human experimentation.

In *On Justices*, Chapter 14 deals with commercial subjects, including employment. In that chapter, Topic 66 is titled Partnerships. In Partnerships, the wages and other costs of sacrifice are regulated in some detail.[65] The rules protect the financial interests of the sacrificers and ensure the sacrifice is completed on behalf of the patron.

It is not a far stretch to analogize the *Vedic* sacrifice to the sacrifices privileged and institutionalized in the neoliberal pharmaceutical sector.

Regarding the sacrifice made by the individual, he or she is both patron and thing being sacrificed. The emphasis of the rule on the sacrifice being completed suggests the state is interested in maintaining the integrity of the sacrificial transaction. Since, on this view, sacrifices are known to work and are such an integral part of day-to-day life, the suggestion is that the institutional misleading of the patron as to the true nature of the sacrifice (it is not therapeutic and it will not result in the common good) would be prohibited. In theory, this is done today with the informed consent process, but it is clear institutional pressures nullify the informed consent generally speaking.

Regarding the sacrifices by the pharmaceutical company and the state, the rules' emphasis on the transactional aspects of the sacrifice suggests that industry would be much more tightly regulated. In other words, the *Arthasastra* envisions a relationship between the state, the citizens and industry that is different from that institutionalized in the neoliberal political order. Here, the state would exercise more control over the financial transactions at the heart of the research enterprise. This could go as far, perhaps, given the centrality of sacrifice to the public, as regulating human experimentation as a utility, setting profit margins and prohibiting or limiting monopolies on medical treatments, devices and drugs. Additionally, it could confer greater power on the individual sacrificers/subjects to negotiate as cohorts for participation or shares in the profits of the drug and set fees, and other benefits subjects could be paid for participation, perhaps based on risk, etc.

About international relations, such as a human rights regime in which the rights of citizens are regulated between kingdoms, it is probably unlikely under the principles of international relations set out in the *Arthasastra*.[66] The *Arthasastra* posits a sixfold strategy in international relations. The first principle is the peace pact. If the conditions exist for a peace treaty, then typical issues addressed in the pact would be land, allies, money and projects. This suggests openings for discussion of trade in drugs but recalling the drug trade would not be anything like our trade now, which is already subject to many international, transnational and global agreements. Perhaps, an agricultural compact to grow certain herbs (i.e. drugs) could be envisioned.

Conclusion

The foregoing analysis answers, with a yes, whether Hinduism has any ideas to offer the contemporary regulation/policy of human experimentation. However, that affirmative answer comes only after the question is unpacked and after considerable historical translation of ideas and explanation of the unpacked question. In summary, it seems to envision a more tightly regulated pharmaceutical industry performing experiments on subjects that have been given much more agency.

Whether the norms expressed in the *Arthasastra* can be considered religious is complicated. The centrality of sacrifice to the householder who adheres to *Vedic* norms is indisputable and could be described as religious since, for example, sacrifices are made to deities, etc. Moreover, even in *moksha dharma*, a *dharma* reflected throughout the cultures and traditions of the subcontinent in its more abstract forms, the notion of sacrifice is important, albeit not as a physical rite. However, the *Arthasastra* is decidedly secular and suggests throughout that religion could be used, for example, as a pretence for covert political activity. That suggests the central concern of the rules is to maintain civic order, not to institutionalize a religion.

Notes

1 Walter Beals, Harold L. Sebring, and Johnson T. Crawford, "Justices," *Judgement* (August 20, 1947). Trial of War Criminals Before the Nuremberg Military Tribunals Under Control Council Law No. 10, Vol. 2 ("The Medical Case") (Washington, DC: United States Government Printing Office, 1948), 181–182, www.loc.gov/rr/frd/Military_Law/pdf/NT_war-criminals_Vol-II.pdf, accessed May 20, 2021. There were earlier norms, particularly in Germany, but they cannot be said to have become universal in any sense of the word. Jay Katz, *Experimentation with Human Beings*, 305 (Russell Sage Foundation, 1972), 284–292.
2 Jay Katz, "The Nuremberg Code and the Nuremberg Trial: A Reappraisal," *JAMA* 276, no. 20 (1996): 1662–1666, at 1665.
3 Samuel Moyn, *The Last Utopia: Human Rights in History* (Cambridge: Belknap Press of Harvard University Press, 2010).

4 U.N. General Assembly, *International Covenant on Civil and Political Rights* (December 16, 1966), United Nations, Treaty Series, vol. 999, 171, www.refworld.org/docid/3ae6b3aa0.html, accessed May 18, 2019, Art. 7.
5 Moyn, *Utopia*. In the 1950s, the World Medical Association (WMA) and the Council for International Organizations of Medical Sciences (CIOMS) enunciated norms requiring consent, but these norms did not even have the force of soft law at the time. Later, they would become elements of a soft law regarding consent and give content to the ICCPR Art 7 positive law.
6 That is, through custom, state practice, *opinio juris*, and other mechanisms, including positive law. Jordan J. Paust, "Customary International Law: Its Nature, Sources and Status as Law of the United States," *Mich. J. Int'l L.* 12 (1990): 59, 59–77. http://repository.law.umich.edu/mjil/vol12/iss1/2. See also Roozbeh (Rudy) B. Baker, "Customary International Law in the 21st Century: Old Challenges and New Debates," *European Journal of International Law* 21, no. 1 (2010): 173–204.
7 See Makau W. Mutua, "The Ideology of Human Rights," *Virginia Journal of International Law* 36, no. 3 (1996): 589. https://digitalcommons.law.buffalo.edu/articles/572. Moreover, in 2019, three of the five seats on the United Nations Security Council are held by states (United States, Russia, and China) that are steadily becoming more nationalistic. Numerous other states, such as Hungary, Poland, the Philippines, and India, are steadily becoming more nationalistic too. This nationalism has acted to severely erode the notion of universal international law, not only in the realm of human rights but also in the more sacrosanct global economic order.
8 Peter Das, "Hinduism in Bioethics," *Encyclopedia of Bioethics*, 4th ed., ed. Bruce Jennings (New York: Macmillan Reference USA, 2014), 1523. See also, Peter Das, "On 'Hindu' Bioethics," in *Saṁskṛta-sādhutā: Goodness of Sanskrit. Studies in Honour of Professor Ashok N. Aklujkar*, ed. Chikafumi Watanabe, Michele Desmarais, and Yoshichika Honda (New Delhi, India: D. K. Printworld, 2012).
9 But see, Wendy Doniger, *The Hindus: An Alternative History* (Oxford: Oxford University Press, 2010) (noting earlier, but incidental, use of the word "Hindu" in a religious sense).
10 See Iza R. Hussin, *The Politics of Islamic Law: Local Elites, Colonial Authority, and the Making of the Muslim State* (Chicago: University of Chicago Press, 2016), 92–95.
11 Das, *Hinduism*.
12 Kautilya, *Arthasastra: King, Governance and Law in Ancient India*, trans. Patrick Olivelle (New York: Oxford University Press, 2013).
13 The explanatory text of Article 25 states that a reference to Hindus includes a reference to Jains, Buddhists and Sikhs. Subsequent Supreme Court cases have recognized this inclusiveness and ambiguity of the word Hindu as referring to a religious affiliation. See Das, *Hinduism*.
14 See, e.g., Narges Mahaluxmivala, "Human Subject Protection in India:—Is It Adequate?," *Perspectives in Clinical Research* 1, no. 1 (2010): 15–20.
15 Ari Altstedter and Anna Edney, "Culture of 'Bending Rules' in India Challenges U.S. Drug Agency," *The Economic Times* (January 31, 2019), https://economictimes.indiatimes.com/industry/healthcare/biotech/pharmaceuticals/culture-of-bending-rules-in-india-challenges-u-s-drug-agency/articleshow/67769847.cms.

94 John Lunstroth

16 These texts and their norms only applied to the elite Sanskrit speakers and their circles. Doniger, *The Hindus*.
17 That is, there are three textual traditions in which texts are drafted and collected under the relevant *purusartha* (purpose), *kama*, *artha* and *dharma*. Wendy Doniger, *Against Dharma: Dissent in the Ancient Indian Sciences of Sex and Politics* (New Haven: Yale University Press, 2018), 1–23.
18 See Alain Daniélou, *The Complete Kama Sutra: The First Unabridged Modern Translation of the Classic Indian Text* (1993).
19 See Kautilya, *Arthasastra*.
20 See Patrick Olivelle (trans.), *The Law Code of Manu (Manava Dharmasastra)* (New York: Oxford University Press, 2004). A central text of the *dharmasastra* tradition.
21 Swami Nikhilananda (trans.), *The Upanishads (With Notes, Explanations and Commentary Based on the Interpretations of Sankaracharya)*, Vol. 4 (New York: Ramakrishna-Vivekananda Centre, 1949–1959).
22 George Thibaut, *Vedanta Sutras Parts 1 & 2*, The Sacred Books of the East at Google Books, Vols. 34 and 38, ed. Max Muller (Oxford: Oxford University Press, 1904).
23 *The Bhagavad-Gita*, trans. Georg Feuerstein, 2011.
24 An additional central text on *moksha dharma* is Patanjali's Yoga Sutras, of which there are numerous translations. See *Yoga-Sutras of Patanjali with the Exposition of Vyasa: A Translation and Commentary*, Vols. 1 and 2, trans. Swami Veda Bharati (India: Himalayan Institute, 1986); Swami Hariharananda Āraṇya, *Yoga philosophy of Patanjali*, trans. P.N. Mukerji (Albany, NY: State University of New York Press, 1983).
25 As a *purusartha*, *dharma* means to do the right thing. This is a procedural norm, though, and it does not convey enough information to know what the right thing is. To know substantive right, one has to know the purpose of the norm (*dharma*), and the purpose is inscribed in the other *purusarthas*, *kama*, *artha* and *moksha*, which in turn are active variously during the stages of life. For the householder centre of gravity, or *grihastha ashrama*, the purposes are *kama* and *artha*. To lead a fulfilling life as a householder, one lives according to *kama-artha dharma*. To lead a successful life as a renunciate, the other center of gravity of the stages of life (*sannyasin ashrama*), one must also live according to the *dharma*, but in this case, it is *moksha dharma*. The rules required to achieve liberation or *moksha* are radically different from the rules to live as a householder.
26 Nikhilananda, *Upanishads*, Vol. 2, "Hindu Ethics" section, 1–5.
27 Aristotle, *Politics 1253a28–30*, trans. C.D.C. Reeve (Indianapolis, IN: Hackett Publishing Company, 1998), 5.
28 That being said, another interesting project would be to examine the *Vedic Samhitas* (mantras and benedictions), *Brahmanas* (commentaries on rituals, ceremonies and sacrifices) and *Aranyakas* (text on rituals, ceremonies, sacrifices and symbolic-sacrifices) for other possible normative guidance. Because the *Upanishadic* texts of the Vedas are clearly concerned with *moksha*, whereas the rest of the Vedas are concerned with the householder's day-to-day life, they would not be part of this project. Would certain rituals/mantras improve certain medical or drug treatments, e.g.? Since amelioration of negative planetary influences is a Vedic subject, would the astrological chart play a role in determining which mantras and rituals would be performed to avoid treatment altogether or ensure its success, etc.? How could that knowledge be used in human experiments?

29 See Kautilya, *Arthasastra*. The history of the science of *artha* and *Kautilya's Arthasastra* is intimately bound to the history of the science of *dharma* and *dharma* texts. Doniger, *Against Dharma*, 11–13. The Arthasastra, in other words, is about the *dharma* of *artha*.
30 See, e.g., Katz, *Experiments*, 176, 291, 731, 735; National Commission for the Protection of Human Subjects of Biomedical and Behavioral Research, *The Belmont Report: Ethical Principles and Guidelines for the Protection of Human Subjects of Research* (Bethesda, MD: The Commission, 1978). See also, Hans Jonas, "Philosophical Reflections on Experimenting with Human Subjects," *Daedalus* 98, no. 2 (1969): 219–247.
31 See Katz, *Experiments*.
32 *Belmont Report*.
33 Pope Pius XII, "The Moral Limits of Medical Research and Treatment," in *Proceedings of the First International Congress of Neuropathology*, Acta Apostolicae Sedis 44 (Rome, 1952), 779–787. (Tran. NCWC News Service), as cited in Katz, *Experiment*, 731–733.
34 Katz, *Experiment*, 732.
35 See John Locke, *Two Treatises of Government*, §2.110, ed. P. Laslett (Cambridge: Cambridge University Press, 1988/1689).
36 Joseph A. DiMasi, Henry G. Grabowski, and Ronald W. Hansen, "Innovation in the Pharmaceutical Industry: New Estimates of R&D Costs," *Journal of Health Economics* 47 (2016): 20–33; Jerry Avorn, "The $2.6 Billion Pill:—Methodologic and Policy Considerations," *New England Journal of Medicine* 372, no. 20 (2015): 1877–1879.
37 Vinsay Prasad and Sham Mailankody, "Research and Development Spending to Bring a Single Cancer Drug to Market and Revenues after Approval," *JAMA Internal Medicine* 177, no. 11 (2017): 1569–1575.
38 Matej Mikulic, "Global Pharmaceutical Industry:—Statistics & Facts," *Statista.com* (November 5, 2020), www.statista.com/topics/1764/global-pharmaceutical-industry/, accessed May 12, 2021; Mary Ellen Biery, "The Most Profitable Industries in 2016," *Forbes.com* (August 6, 2016), www.forbes.com/sites/sageworks/2016/08/06/the-most-profitable-industries-in-2016/, accessed May 12, 2021.
39 Mikulic, "Global."
40 *Ibid*.
41 L.M. Schwartz and S. Woloshin, "Medical Marketing in the United States, 1997–2016," *JAMA* 321, no. 1 (2019): 80–96.
42 Mikulic, "Global."
43 Included are devices and other treatments such as biologicals.
44 Mikulic, "Global." However, the pharmaceutical industry does not fund basic research that identifies the promising compounds in the U.S. Basic research is funded by the government, which does not participate in the profits of drugs brought to market. Alexander Zaitchik, "Taxpayers:—Not Big Pharma:—Has Funded the Research Behind Every New Drug since 2010," (Spring 2018), https://other98.com/taxpayers-fund-pharma-research-development/, accessed June 3, 2019.
45 Schwartz, *Medical Marketing*.
46 Mikulic, "Global."
47 Valerie Gutmann Koch, "A Private Right of Action for Informed Consent in Research," (April 6, 2014). *Seton Hall Law Review* 45, no. 1 (2015), Chicago-Kent College of Law Research Paper No. 2014–26. Available at SSRN: https://ssrn.com/abstract=2421065.

48 Koch, "A Private Right," 183–193.
49 *Ibid.*
50 Moreover, many ethicists consider it wrong to provide more than a nominal fee, if anything, because it would amount to undue influence, which is explicitly prohibited. Christine Grady, "Payment of Clinical Research Subjects," *The Journal of Clinical Investigation* 115, no. 7 (2005): 1681–1687.
51 Koch, "Private Right." The federal statute authorizing and regulating human experimentation does not confer an individual cause of action in injured subjects. Rather it authorizes the Office of Human Research Protections to ban or otherwise punish researchers and institutions that cause injuries.
52 *Oxford English Dictionary*, 2nd ed. (Oxford: Oxford University Press, 2004), s.v. "Sacrifice," at https://en.oxforddictionaries.com/definition/sacrifice. See generally, Henri Hubert and Marcel Mauss, *Sacrifice: Its Nature and Function*, trans. W.D. Halls (Chicago: University of Chicago Press, 1981); Rene Girard, *Violence and the Sacred*, trans. Patrick Gregory (Baltimore and London: Johns Hopkins University Press, 1979); Walter Burkert, *Homo Necans: The Anthropology of Ancient Greek Sacrificial Ritual and Myth*, trans. Peter Bing (Berkley: University of California Press, 1983).
53 Larry Churchill, "Therapeutic Misconception (T.M.) in Clinical Research," (June 2013), www.mc.vanderbilt.edu/crc/workshop_files/2013-06-21.ppt, accessed July 5, 2019.
54 Robert Langreth, "Drug Prices," *Bloomberg* (February 5, 2019), www.bloomberg.com/quicktake/drug-prices, accessed June 5, 2019.
55 Nikhilananda, *The Upanishads*, Vol. 1, 7–8.
56 See Doninger, *Against Dharma*, 8–13.
57 Kautilya, *Arthasastra*, 29. See also Doniger, *Against Dharma*, noting the latest emendations to the text were made in the 4th century C.E.
58 See Olivelle, *The Law Code of Manu*.
59 The following description is taken from Nikhilananda, *Upanishads*, 2–4. However, these are some of the oldest texts in existence and parts of them are still widely in use in India and among the diaspora, and their complexity cannot be underestimated. For an introduction, see Wikipedia contributors, "Vedas," *Wikipedia: The Free Encyclopedia*, https://en.wikipedia.org/w/index.php?title=Vedas&oldid=890019870, accessed May 27, 2019.
60 Of note is that human sacrifice can be found in the Vedic texts. See Anonymous, *Truth about Hinduism*, https://vedkabhed.wordpress.com/2014/02/16/purushamedha-the-human-sacrifice/ (quoting exact citations in the Vedas).
61 Kautilya, *Arthasastra*, 179–222.
62 *Ibid.*, 109–111.
63 There are numerous references under the entries for physicians and medicines in the index of the Arthasastra.
64 See Dominik Wujastyk (trans.), *The Roots of Ayruveda: Selections from Sanskrit Medical Writings* (India: Penguin Books, 1998), xxx. Francesca Bray, "Chinese Medicine," in *Companion Encyclopedia of the History of Medicine*, Vol. 2, ed. Roy Porter and W.F. Bynum (London and New York: Routledge, 1993), 732–734; Samuel Hahnemann, *Organon of Medicine*, 6th ed. (India: B. Jain Publishers, 1992), Aphorisms 1–29.
65 Kautilya, *Arthasastra*, 211–212.
66 Kautilya, *Arthasastra*, 277–330, Book Seven: "On the Six-Fold Strategy."

8 Informed consent and clinical trials

A Jewish perspective

David Heyd

Clinical trials started no more than 150 years ago. Informed consent is an even more recent moral principle in medical practice. Accordingly, it is no surprise that the Jewish tradition (like all other religious and ethical systems) consists of no *direct* instruction on these practices. However, it does not mean that the two-and-a-half millennia old corpus of Jewish law is completely silent on the principles which may guide us in modern times in the regulation of experiments on human subjects and the role of individual consent on the part of those participating in them.

It is a second-level methodological principle in the Jewish halakhic tradition that any practical opinion or ruling must be anchored in previous opinions of rabbinical authorities. These, in turn, also rely on earlier rulings and the argumentation supporting them—down to the formative texts of the Talmud and ultimately the Torah, the foundation of all religious authority. One of the most powerful intellectual tools for forming opinions on matters that are novel and never addressed in the past is called *hekesh*, which can be translated as analogy or inference. Analogical thinking is the bridge between the necessity of maintaining the binding authority of past thought and the need to solve entirely new problems which arise in our age.

Take a typical case for the way contemporary rabbis debate the issue of clinical trials and informed consent. They go back to the sixteenth-century authority, Rabbi David ben Zimra, who in one of his thousands of responses to various religious questions discusses the following imaginary case:

> What if the ruler tells a Jew, "let me cut one of your non-vital body parts or I shall kill one of your fellow Jews"? Some say that the Jew must let his organ be cut [thereby saving the life of his friend] since the organ is not vital [like a leg or an eye].[1]

The historical context of this question in the sixteenth century is the experience of such terrible dilemmas faced by members of a persecuted minority

DOI: 10.4324/9781003213215-11

which is, sometimes, the victim of cruel bullying. Strikingly, it became a classical source for rabbinical debates about life-saving organ donation in recent decades and, although more abstractly, about vaccination and participation in clinical trials.[2]

Ben Zimra's opinion is unambiguous: letting the ruler cut part of one's body is *supererogatory*, a matter of charity (*hassidut*), that is to say—going beyond the call of duty or the requirement of the religious law (*din*). This is not a trivial ruling since what is at stake is a person's *life*, which in Jewish law and ethics is the greatest of all values justifying even the violation of the Sabbath or almost all religious commandments. Hence, exempting one from saving the life of another human being calls for special justification, which Ben Zimra is at pains to provide. One kind of reasoning is that the sacrifice of one's limb *may* cause profuse bleeding resulting in death (and then, there is no reason for me to sacrifice my life for another person's life which is not worth more than mine). Another, more principled, the argument is that organs are integral parts of one's life and hence cannot serve as instruments for either punishing a criminal or saving another person's life. The ultimate argument of ben Zimra is that "the way of the Torah is gentle and it is necessary that its judgements agree with reason and commonsense." Can it really be expected, asks ben Zimra, that a person would allow his eye to be taken or his hand or leg be cut to save the life of another? Hence, he concludes that it is entirely optional and supererogatory to save one's friend's life by sacrificing a non-vital organ, and he who can bring himself to do it should be blessed. However, adds ben Zimra, if the sacrifice of an organ risks the life of the donor, he should be considered a "foolish" or irrational man (*hassid shoteh*), rather than a virtuous person.

The historical circumstances have changed: no ruler nowadays poses a threat "let me cut your hand, or I will kill your friend." Now the threat is "get vaccinated, or some people in your community will die in an epidemic." But, the normative dilemma remains the same: must an individual make some physical sacrifice to save other people's lives in the community.[3] On the one hand, the Jewish normative system is typically communitarian, guided by solidarity and mutual responsibility. The social commitment may sometimes make substantial demands on the individual. On the other hand, the individual has a strong duty of *self-care*.[4] The Jewish halakhic tradition wavers between the commitment to the saving of life (often encapsulated in the verse "thou shall not stand idly by")[5] and the recognition that an individual has a special and maybe prior commitment to his *own* life and bodily integrity. There is a whole set of rules regarding the prohibition of self-mutilation, and the rabbis discuss in detail the exceptions which usually have to do with the possible saving of another human life and especially of a family member. But as we shall see, taking part in a clinical trial may be considered self-harm that cannot be justified in terms of the direct utility to an identifiable relative. Ben Zimra takes the middle way in solving this tension: sacrificing a limb for the sake of saving the life of another person is at most an admirable act of pure altruism but never a duty.

Organ donations are closely analogous to these older non-medical dilemmas since they involve a direct life-saving sacrifice of one's limb. But, vaccinations and clinical trials raise similar tensions between the individual duty of self-care and the social commitment to public health, which is a public good. Some vaccinations and some clinical trials involve danger to one's life and health and hence face the same difficulty that besieged Jewish communities in the past had to deal with. There is, though, a significant difference between clinical trials and medical experiments: the former is a practice that aims at preventing concrete threats of infectious disease, which may cause direct harm to a high number of people in the actual community. Medical experiments aim at promoting chances of curing diseases of future people whom we do not know and who may not have even been born yet. In that respect, refusing to be vaccinated and taking a free ride on fellow citizens is unfair and consequently justifies legal enforcement of some form. Medical experiments have a more remote utility and hence nowadays are never forced. Taking part in them is supererogatory.[6] An even more extreme view is presented by the philosopher Hans Jonas who argues that due to their health risks, we should prohibit even volunteers from taking part in dangerous medical experiments and allow only the researchers themselves to undergo the experimental procedure as a matter of professional responsibility or *noblesse oblige*. However, in today's methodologies, Jonas' restriction is unrealistic. We need a very large number of subjects for any clinical trial and hence the cooperation of sick patients and healthy people for a control group. So to what degree should society allow its members to be subject to health risks?

Here, we come to another principle that has guided the rabbis from ancient times—the degree of risk. Naturally, contemporary rabbis are more aware of the importance of probabilities, and their arguments about medical experimentation have become more sophisticated. One significant distinction is between the experimental treatment of a particular sick patient and clinical trials that recruit healthy people.[7] Regarding the treatment of a particular sick person, there is a distinction between a patient whose life is in danger and a patient who suffers from a non-fatal illness. If the threat of death is real and the treatment has some reasonable chance of saving the patient's life, although *some* chance of shortening his life, he is *permitted* (though not obliged) to choose to take the risk of that experimental treatment. It is interesting to note that unlike the older tradition, which did not even raise the issue of the patient's consent and relied entirely on the doctor's judgement, in this contemporary opinion, the patient is asked whether he wishes to take the experimental medication and if "it is impossible to talk about it with the patient" the family should be consulted. Although patient consent was already implied in older opinions of the kind we have discussed earlier in the form of leaving a space of *permission* to people who choose to donate an organ to save the life of another, rabbis in modern rulings explicitly require consultation with and consent of the patient. Furthermore, this applies equally to patients who are not in life danger but are given a chance to recuperate or relieve pain by taking an experimental medication.

As for experiments involving healthy people, these raise again the tension between the duty of self-care and the duty to save the lives of others. Again, there is a distinction between cases in which the other is an actual person "standing in front of me" and an unidentified future person who might enjoy the benefits of the clinical trial. If the actual person has a good chance to be saved from death by my help (blood donation or organ donation) while the risk of death I incur is minimal, then I am allowed to undergo the experimental procedure. However, if those who stand to benefit are future unidentified people (as is the case in most clinical trials), it would be my duty to take part in them *only* if the harm they involve is minimal or non-existent.[8] Experiments on human subjects which are risky and potentially harmful in more significant ways are prohibited, which means that the doctors are not allowed to conduct them, and individuals are barred from volunteering to take part in them. Even informed consent would not legitimize them. The rabbinical ruling here accords with the common bioethical belief that "statistical lives" are not as valuable as the life of actual people (a belief that is challenged by some philosophers who regard this belief as irrational and ethically unsound).[9]

A relatively rigid and "polarized" opinion is expressed by Immanuel Jakobovitz, former chief rabbi of the U.K. and the pioneer of Jewish bioethics in modern times. Jakobovitz argues that, on the one hand, if there is no risk or danger involved in the experiment, we have a positive duty to take part in it; on the other hand, if there is some risk or danger to our health, we are straightforwardly prohibited from partaking in the experiment.[10] This is a conservative view that is not representative of current rabbinical thought. It leaves no room for volunteering since taking part in the clinical trial is either obligatory or prohibited.

A more restrictive opinion is offered by an important rabbinical authority of our age, R. Waldenberg.[11] Taking part in medical experiments should be kept entirely voluntary even if the risk involved is minimal or considered non-existent. One can never know about hidden risks involved in experimentation, and one should also consider the possibility of the unpredicted psychological impact of the procedure on the subject. Furthermore, one can never guarantee that the experiment would yield the expected benefit to future people. In other words, the probability of some harm to the subject taking part in a medical trial is often higher than is commonly thought, and the probability of benefit to future patients too low to justify any social obligation to participate in medical experiments. In my phrasing, Waldenberg's idea is that our bodies cannot serve as instruments for promoting the health of other people.

Although the patient's consent to treatment has not been traditionally considered by the halakha as a condition for medical treatment—particularly in life-and-death situations—donating organs or participating in altruistic clinical trials was either forbidden or left to the free choice of the individual. Note that this is a weak sense of consent. However, under the influence of the rigid condition of informed consent in modern bioethics, we see the rabbis following suit. In one recent response, we find a clear statement: "even if the results of clinical trials are important, it is impossible to force an individual [to take part in them] without his knowledge." It is the doctor's duty to explain to the patient that with his help, human lives can be saved and ask for his consent. It is an offence to experiment on patients without their knowledge and against their will, even if the intention is the hope to cure future patients.[12]

On a more philosophical level, one should note that despite adopting the general idea of informed consent, the Jewish way of thinking does not accept the principle of *autonomy* as the grounds for informed consent. Autonomy is a richer concept than consent. It implies a general view of human beings as masters of their lives, the source of value and moral duty. It is the key notion of the anthropocentric version of humanism. Jewish religious thinking does not consider the individual as sovereign over his own life, and even his body is not considered his property. The requirement of consent in medical treatment is based on the potential suffering and harm to the body and the duty of self-care rather than absolute control of human beings over their lives. Thus, informed consent is not a major principle in the doctor–patient relationship since it is a doctor's duty to heal and a parallel duty of the patient to be healed. Being cured is not a matter of choice or personal autonomy.

However, when it comes to taking part in clinical trials, in which *other* people are the beneficiaries, there is no such duty (to be healed), and the individual must be asked to express his genuine consent before being recruited.[13] Or take experiments on minors. They are prohibited because children cannot give consent to a procedure that might cause them pain or undermine their health. But, according to some rabbinical authorities, such experiments are allowed if they do not involve any suffering or risks to the child. This opinion conflicts with the liberal principle of autonomy, requiring consent even when there is no risk or pain involved in the experimental procedure. Consider the well-known danger of giving too much information to the patient (in either medical treatment or the recruitment of subjects for a clinical trial): as research has shown, too much information may disrupt the rational deliberation of the patient giving the consent, thereby undermining his autonomy. How do we know when autonomy is undermined? For the Jewish approach, restricting the amount of information given to the subject does not pose a problem since it is sufficient for the doctor to be convinced that extra information might cause unnecessary anxiety and suffering to the patient. The liberal, autonomy-based approach requires that all potential participants in the trial be given the *same* amount of information. The Jewish, consent-based attitude allows for different amounts of information to different subjects based on their degree of anxiety.

We can now see why the general attitude of contemporary halakha is compatible with the principles of the Helsinki Convention although its theoretical basis is different from the liberal principles underlying that Convention. Consequently, the legal regulation of experimentation on human subjects in Israel does not encounter any obstacle on the part of religious circles or parties. The Helsinki Convention is accepted as the supreme guiding document in the ethics of experimentation, and a Helsinki committee in each research hospital is a statutory legal requirement. But again, this does not mean that religious authorities accept the practice in the liberal terms of rights, autonomy and informed consent. They instead appeal to the principles of the sanctity of life, the duty of self-care, social solidarity and the value of bodily integrity.

How do all these developments in religious discussion of clinical trials, vaccinations and informed consent affect the actual way in which the orthodox religious sectors behave regarding those practices? There is a lower rate of immunization in the ultra-orthodox sector of Israeli society, but the cause for that phenomenon is not easy to detect. Indeed, there were a few cases in which leading rabbis instructed their communities to avoid immunization, but this occurred on the occasion of some medical controversy about the effectiveness of particular immunization (which also led some non-religious sectors to refuse to immunize their children). There is some general suspicion from these communities regarding the State and the Ministry of Health instructions. This suspicion is not derived from any formal religious argument against the idea of immunization as such. Living in small and relatively isolated communities, this sector in the population may feel that the "herd effect" of most people getting immunized is sufficient to protect them from the disease without them taking the inoculation.

Furthermore, some immunizations are thought of as conveying a negative moral message, such as the inoculation against papillomavirus, preventing cervical cancer in young women. However, beyond these sociologically relevant explanations, I should emphasize that the leading religious authorities do not oppose immunization, and many of them strongly encourage their followers, including children, to take them. Some consider them and clinical trials even as "a holy war" against the threat of fatal illness, a war that calls for a universal draft.

The issue then is not informed consent. Nor is it a problem of dietary restrictions (*kashrut*). Ultra-orthodox people—even though they can understand informed consent forms and the terminology used in them—need the authority of the rabbis to get involved in practices that might create a religious problem. For them, taking part in clinical trials or an immunization program is a matter of *legitimacy* rather than *autonomy*. We could say that their consent is *mediated* through the rabbis. Hence, as a matter of state policy, the medical community must convey to the rabbinical authorities state-of-the-art information about effective and experimental treatments so that the rabbis can lend their authority to individuals who hesitate to opt for them. The small minority of ultra-orthodox communities in Israel (and abroad) is not a case of a *vulnerable* group, but rather that of a group that should be encouraged by its religious leaders to join a highly profitable health scheme that their leaders recognize to be so. Mediated consent is the most effective means of creating trust conditions, which is a key to the success of experimental and preventive programs, indeed, to medical practice in general.

Notes

1 R. David ben Zimra, *Responsa*, part 3, section 627. My translation. Responsa are the most common medium in the development of halakhic rulings. They are written replies by a rabbi or a Talmudic scholar to inquiries on any matter of Jewish law. They are usually collected in volumes authored by either the rabbi himself or later by his pupils. They serve as rulings for the community of that rabbi and as opinions to be considered by later scholars engaged in the same inquiry.
2 I first encountered this source in a seminar paper of a student of mine, Noam Shar'abi, on the subject of organ donations.
3 There is a famous Talmudic dilemma: should the enemy command the community to hand over one of its members to be killed or otherwise be *all* put to death—what should the community do? The received answer is that the community should avoid sacrificing one individual and be prepared to be completely wiped out. However, if the enemy identifies the wanted individual, *he* should be handed over. By way of analogy, one might argue that if a particular individual contracted a highly infectious disease, he could be removed from the city, even if that means that he will die. However, if one person should be arbitrarily selected to take part in some lethal medical experiment that might save the whole community, it would be strictly prohibited to force him to undergo that experiment (although as in the case of the wanted individual, he will anyway die with the whole group). See *Jerusalem Talmud*, Tractate *Terumot*, p. 47a.

4 "For your own sake, therefore, be most careful" (Deuteronomy 4:15). This verse was given in later ages its current physical meaning, including the duty to be healed by getting medical treatment.
5 Leviticus 19:16. This strong commandment to save the life of another person is unambiguously asserted by Maimonides, in his *Mishne Torah*, "Rotzeach uShmirat Nefesh," chapter 1, section 14: "Whenever a person can save another person's life, but he fails to do so, he transgresses a negative commandment, as Leviticus 19:16 states: "Do not stand idly by while your brother's blood is at stake."
6 Nevertheless, despite the authority of ben Zimra on the matter, there are some contemporary rabbis who—being aware of the immediate threats of certain new epidemics (say, AIDS)—view medical experimentation as "a holy war" ("a war of duty"), in which, according to the Torah, everybody is under a duty to take part. This is a more dramatic way of giving clinical trials a religious value. See, for example, M.D. Wellner, "The Rights and Authority of the Physician," in *Hatora ve'Hamedina* [The Torah and the State], Vol. 8, ed. Shaul Yisraeli (Kfar Haroeh, 1956–7), 306–307, 312. [In Hebrew].
7 Avraham Sofer Avraham, *Nishmat Avraham*, part 3, section 349 (Jerusalem: A.S. Sofer, 1985). The author is not a religious authority but a religious physician writing on bioethical issues.
8 Avraham Sofer Avraham, "Experiments on Human Subject," *Noam: An Annual for the Discussion of Halakhic Problems* 17 (1964): 161–164. [In Hebrew] The view expressed here is slightly different from that expressed in his other book cited earlier.
9 In his handy *Encyclopedia for Halakha and Medicine* (Jerusalem: Schlesinger Institute, 1994), Avraham Steinberg quotes R. Shlomo Zalman Auerbach as ruling that one is under no duty to save the life of another even if it involves no risk; but one is permitted to do so. However, it is prohibited to take part in an experiment that is risky to one's life. But, adds the rabbi, it may be allowed if the person to be saved from death is "standing in front of us," i.e., an identifiable concrete individual desperate to be saved. Entry "Medical Experiments on Human Subjects" (Vol. 7), p. 490.
10 Immanuel Jakobovitz, *Jewish Medical Ethics* (New York: Bloch Publishing Company, 1975), 291–294. Although the book's first edition was published before the Helsinki Convention in 1964, the second edition was published quite a while after it but, in a way, ignores it.
11 R. Eliezer Waldenberg, *Tzitz Eliezer* [Responsa], 2nd ed., Vol. 13, section 101 (Jerusalem, 1985). Waldenberg (1915–2006) was one of the foremost authorities on religious medical ethics.
12 Moshe Sternbuch, *Teshuvot ve'Hanhagot* [response], part 1, section 895 (Jerusalem: Netivot ha'Torah ve'Hachesed, 1992).
13 Yechiel Michael Barilan, *Jewish Bioethics* (Cambridge: Cambridge University Press, 2014), 119–122.

9 Christian perspectives on informed consent

Laura Palazzani

Informed consent: general ethical principle from the Christian perspective

The Christian perspective in bioethics, in the framework of a creationistic concept of nature with a normative value (finalism) and in a belief to know the truth in nature (cognitivism), considers human life as worthy of respect and protection (as a gift from God and created in His image) since it is the expression of personal life, dynamically intent on fully manifesting itself.

The principles proposed in bioethics are the following: *the defence of human life*'s objective and absolute value, its intangibility and the impossibility to dispose of it arbitrarily; the *therapeutic principle*, according to which any intervention on life is justifiable only if it aims to cure the subject (to save lives and improve health); the *principle of freedom and responsibility*, where freedom denotes an objective limit to respect the lives of others; the *principle of justice and solidarity* or attaining common good through the good of the individual and solidarity towards those in need according to their particular vulnerabilities.[1]

Informed consent acquires a specific meaning in this conceptual framework. The Catholic Medical Association and National Catholic Bioethics Centre published a document entitled "Catholic Principles and Guidelines for Clinical Research,"[2] which made references to the concept of informed consent in both clinical practice and research. The basic understanding of Christianity regarding informed consent is

1 *The physician's duty to inform* and tell the truth in a complete, clear and comprehensible way about the health of the patient and the possibility to be cured (prevention, diagnosis and therapy) and cared for. The physician should be neither directive nor descriptive/neutral towards the patients but *help them make conscious decisions oriented towards proportionate protection and respect for life*. There is no place for

DOI: 10.4324/9781003213215-12

intentional falsehoods, misleading statements or bias. It is the responsibility of everyone, especially a physician or a medical researcher, to respect the sacred and inviolable right to life of the human subject at every stage from its first formation to death. In this regard, the obligations of the natural moral law and Catholic moral teaching must always be respected. The medical researcher and those who assist in medical research must strive to do good (principle of beneficence) and avoid causing deliberate harm to the subjects in any possible way (principle of non-maleficence).

2   *The duty of the patient to be informed to be aware of the decision.* When there is a trusting relationship with the physician (a sort of "conscious paternalism" requested by the patient), there may also be a right not to be informed in specific circumstances. In both cases, the Christian perspective emphasizes the duty *to accept the cure and care of the physician.* In this sense, the patient's conscious, free and autonomous choice is respectful of life's value when it is orientated towards the objective good: the conservation of life and health improvement by accepting appropriate treatment. In the case of minors and those who lack the capacity to consent (incapacitated), either parents or surrogates may offer decision-making according to their best objective interests. The priority of the objective value of life is derived from the natural law precepts to conserve life. In this context, there may be a difference between the Protestant (more open to subjectivity) and the Catholic perspectives (more linked to the objectivity of the ethical choice).[3]

3   Informed consent for both the physician or health professional and the patient should (in a framework of *human dignity and personal integrity*) *respect the principles of beneficence (priority of the good for the patient) and non-maleficence (not to harm the patient).* These principles refer to the criterion of risk–benefit proportionality: the potential (direct or indirect) benefits of any study must be weighed against potential risks (concerning integrity, health and well-being). When a particular intervention does not directly benefit a minor or members of a vulnerable population, the associated risks must be relatively insignificant (a burden, reduced to a minimum). Research against the good of the person is immoral. High risk is unacceptable. Adequately verifying all the benefits and risks involved in the intervention is essential.

4   In this respect, *the principle of responsibility* should guide the choice of both the patient and the physician. The physician has therapeutic responsibility towards the patient, and the patient or subject has personal responsibility towards one's life and health and social responsibility for the good of science and society. Regardless of physical-psychic or social condition or medical need, everyone must be fully and adequately

protected as a person worthy of respect. Generally, both the human subject and the researcher must recognize the moral obligations under natural law deriving from the value of life and be responsible for it.[4]

5 *The principle of autonomy.* The physician must respect the spirituality and religious beliefs of the human subject. The physician should not compromise these beliefs without failing in some moral duty of the natural law. If the patient refuses an appropriate treatment (or asks for inappropriate treatments), the physician should try to convince him to be cured but cannot impose his view. Conversely, in case of a confident refusal, grounded in religious or rational/emotional motivations, he needs to accept it. Verbal coercion or forceful persuasion is not acceptable. However, based on the assumption that patients are, sometimes, in too much pain and are not objective enough to make the right moral decision, medical staff and family members can withhold certain information and persuade the patient to make the best moral choice. Free and informed consent should not be individualistic as if the patient were an isolated decision-maker. Instead, it should embed the patient in a relational context that supports and properly orients his choices. He or his surrogate should have access to medical and moral information and counselling to form her conscience. Free and informed healthcare decisions should be followed if they do not contradict Catholic principles. If a request for treatment goes against the moral conscience of the physician, he could object (*conscientious objection*). The medical researcher has the moral responsibility to act with a properly formed conscience and withdraw from a scientific intervention or investigation rather than act against his judgement of conscience.

6 Informed consent is inspired by Jesus, who cured the sick *with compassion, generosity, and understanding*. Christians believe that disease and suffering are trials from God to bring them closer to salvation through the death and into His grace. Scientific research should be done to serve those who are ill, not solely or primarily for the benefit of the researchers. Research should be conducted according to accepted scientific principles, and it should be deemed necessary and potentially useful for the patient. We cannot subject an individual to unnecessary or disproportionate risks which exceed the research's expected benefit. The researcher must never participate in projects that may involve treating the human subject as an object of interest. Studies that may involve immoral cooperation with evil must be avoided. The subjects may choose to accept risks or sacrifice themselves (especially in experimentations where risks are higher) for the good of others and society out of solidarity or charity. However, we need to protect the subject's

integrity by verifying authentic intention and the absence of any coercion or pressure.

In this perspective,

> The Church respects and supports scientific research when it has a genuinely humanist orientation, avoiding any form of instrumentalization or destruction of the human being and keeping itself free from the slavery of political and economic interests. In presenting the moral orientations dictated by natural reason, the Church is convinced that she offers a precious service to scientific research, doing her utmost for the true good of the human person. In this perspective, she recalls that, not only the aims, but also the methods and means of research must always respect the dignity of every human being, at every stage of his development and in every phase of experimentation.[5]

Informed consent and conditions of vulnerability

The *principle of precaution/prudence is generally applied in the Christian perspective. Above all, it must be applied in case of conditions of vulnerability* because of the severity of the illness, age (minors, elderly), sex (men/women), socio-cultural conditions (indigent, immigrants).[6]

Informed consent of the incapable person and minors

In the case of minors who are legally not capable of understanding and making decisions, their involvement is justified by a proportionality between the foreseeable risks and benefits in the framework of good and relevant research. Experimentation that is not expected to provide direct benefits for the minor, but only for other persons in similar conditions (in terms of age, type of illness and other characteristics), can be ethically justified when it is not possible to obtain the same results through experiments on adult, competent subjects and the risks and burdens are minimal.[7]

On the basis of the principle of equality and justice, just like any other human being, children have the right to receive drugs that will guarantee health in the same way adults do. It would not be ethical to exclude children from trials since it would mean discriminating against their interests and fundamental rights to life and health.

One of the most critical elements of clinical trials in children is informed consent. The need to obtain the consent of both parents is an established bioethical practice. Concerning the general information before consent, the investigator must evaluate the parents' real motives to accept their child's recruitment in a trial and exclude ethically unacceptable reasons. For example, to benefit from medical treatment that is otherwise not guaranteed or obtain greater attention by the doctors in the treatment of the children.

The parents' consent should be accompanied by the child's assent, which is proof of their actual involvement in the medical decisions, together with their parents. The appropriateness of the information will be evaluated case by case according to cultural and social context and the existential context since each child has a different evolution and maturity and can react differently to illness or pain.

The minor should receive information from expert personnel proportional to their capacity to understand the risks and benefits according to age and maturity. Furthermore, the investigator should consider the desire expressed by the minor to take part in the experimentation or withdraw from it at any moment. The child should be told that their desires are important in the decision, making it clear that they cannot be decisive alone. Specific attention should be paid so that the child's involvement is not an indirect insistence on participation, which should always be free and unconditioned by external factors. The conditioning is particularly problematic in a paediatric phase given the child's vulnerability from the external influences of adults, members of the family and doctors. In the context of assent, doctors should help the child to understand the aim of the trial, the procedures forthcoming and the experiences that they will have. They should try to perceive how much the child has understood and what are their often-unexpressed concerns are to help participants to overcome them. The best interests of the children is the principal Christian value in clinical practice and research.

A challenging element is the involvement of healthy or sick children as a control group or as subjects of "non-therapeutic" experimentation. They will not receive any direct benefits but only indirect ones by helping other children with identical pathology in the future. Non-therapeutic experimentation on minors cannot be excluded if significant improvements in scientific knowledge were to be achieved with a positive willingness and minimum risk or discomfort.

Disputes exist among Catholic moral theologians and bioethicists about whether proxy consent can ever be morally valid in non-therapeutic settings and, if it can, under what conditions and why. One of the most debated issues regards the concepts of minimal risk and discomfort in non-therapeutic research. Is it licit to subject the incompetent persons to non-therapeutic procedures involving minimal risk or a risk slightly exceeding minimal? If so, what benchmarks should be employed? If not, would any amount of risk in non-therapeutic experimentation render it morally objectionable? What degree of risk can be justified in non-therapeutic settings, and how is the risk–benefit ratio determined in each case? There is a need for a careful justification of the scientific relevance of the study and a detailed reflection on informed consent in Catholic anthropological and moral premises, which give priority to the dignity of the human person.[8]

In this context, it is indispensable that informed assent/consent exists regarding the risk and the entity of the risk. Christian perspective considers it legitimate to perform a non-therapeutic trial on a child with an actual capacity of informed assent and supported by the consent of the parents or legal representatives if there are no significant risks either for the life or for the physical integrity of the minor. The requisite of the minimum risk and or discomfort is ethically central.

It is a different bioethical evaluation to use experimental drugs as a last resort to save a minor's life with incurable terminal conditions (maybe also in a condition of imminent death) and in the absence of effective therapeutic alternatives. In such cases, the ethical decision should be proportionate to the actual circumstances to seek the conditions that are respectful of the dignity of the minor. In the first place, it is essential to gather objective scientific data about the seriousness of the illness (verification of the condition of impossibility of cure). Second, we need to consider the present and foreseeable future suffering, the patient's quality of life and the reduction of suffering.

Experimental pharmacological interventions which are aggressive and intensive are ethically licit and proper in the Christian perspective when there is a minimum "therapeutic hope" and when the likely suffering is proportionate to the potential benefits to improve the quality of life (or at least minimization of suffering), with the consent of the parents and possibly the assent of the minors. The suspension of aggressive and intensive experimental therapies is ethically licit and, sometimes, dutiful when life expectancy is short, the prognosis is undoubtedly poor and the therapies futile and harmful. In these cases of so-called therapeutic obstinacy, only ordinary treatment is given along with palliative care and human caregiving. Human and Christian solidarity justifies these gestures and gives them meaning and value.

Research on women: informed consent of fertile, pregnant and breastfeeding women

There are different reasons for underrepresentation and numerical inferiority of participation of women in clinical trials. Some reasons generally concern the way of considering experimentation and medicine. In experimentation, there is a tendency towards "generalization," a tendency towards "neutrality" and assimilation of women to men. These orientations conflict with the need for individual specification and gender differentiation, above all today, in the time of the so-called precision medicine.[9]

The possible pregnancy in childbearing age has led the pharmaceutical companies to exclude women from clinical protocols or impose specific hormonal contraceptives as a condition for participation in research because of the possible risks to the foetus.

From the Christian perspective, if clinical trials endanger the foetus's life or health recognized as a subject of rights, it is ethically preferable for women not to participate when such risks exceed the potential benefits to the women. Suppose the woman decides to enrol in the trial for social or personal aims. In that case, she should, nevertheless, be able to choose the modalities freely and responsibly to avoid pregnancy following her values and religious beliefs, among which abstinence from sexual relations, insofar as she should deem the use of contraceptives illicit owing to the scission between unitive act and procreation (as in the Catholic perspective). Using contraception also raises the problem of contra-gestation, which may impede not only the fecundation of gamete but also the process of implantation.

This particularly thorny issue requires a bioethical analysis that balances the needs of the trial with the values of the subjects taking part in the experimentation. The Christian bioethics perspective of informed consent will consider the gender difference and the moral principles of those taking part in the trials, offering women the possibility of sexual abstinence. If it is incompatible with the trial protocols, women will receive appropriate consultation to choose responsibly according to their moral and religious values. Informed consent should also be undersigned by her partner and include a variable time frame that can be extended even after the trial.[10]

Another specific bioethical issue in clinical research involves pregnant women. In this context, physicians often prescribe drugs for pregnant and breastfeeding women without studies or evidence of safety and efficacy under those conditions. Such treatments may include medications that can cause serious harm for both the woman and the foetus. The exclusion of pregnant women from clinical trials is the cause of the lack of data on potential benefits and harms to women and their future children. Therefore, we need to design research protocols for pregnant and breastfeeding women to determine potential risks and benefits.

Clinical research on pregnant women needs specific ethical requirements. Research with a potential direct benefit is only allowed when it cannot be carried out on non-pregnant and non-breastfeeding women. Risk–benefit assessment must consider the specific pregnancy situation, extend it to foetuses and even include the preconception staged. In such research, the criteria of minimal risk and minimum burden are compulsory for both the woman and the child. "Minimal risk" refers to the degree of harm or discomfort which should not be greater than those experienced in daily life or routine physical or psychological examinations. Research ethics committees require specific attention and prudence. In any event, evidence from prior animal experimentation is necessary.[11]

According to the Christian perspective, pregnant or breastfeeding women should not participate in non-therapeutic research that carries more than minimal risk to them and the foetus or infant unless the experiment is intended to explain pregnancy or lactation problems when there are no alternatives. When the research during pregnancy carries more than minimal risk, the woman should participate in follow-up evaluations to assess the effects on her and her foetus or child. She should be informed of the risks that participation may have on her health and the embryo, foetus and infant. If new scientific information arises during the research, this information should be immediately given to participants. At any stage of the research, the subject's right to withdraw consent should be respected. Follow-up of the pregnancy, the foetus and the child is essential, even months after the study.

Research in a multicultural setting: intercultural informed consent

Special attention must be given to vulnerable persons in clinical experimentation because of dependence (students, prisoners, military service personnel), social insecurity or poverty (the homeless, the unemployed, immigrants) and lack of education. These vulnerable situations could make it difficult to obtain valid informed consent.

Research carried out in emerging or developing countries should have clinical and scientific objectives that directly and specifically concern the local population. The scientific and ethical criteria used to evaluate and conduct these experiments must be the same as those conducted in developed countries. This research must respect local traditions and cultures and be approved in advance by either a national ethics committee of the sponsoring country or the local ethics committee. Researchers may carry out clinical experiments, especially those dealing with severe pathologies with no proven treatment. Experimental treatments could also involve women and men of childbearing potential, with possible risks when pregnancy occurs.[12]

Applying general ethical standards of clinical trials to the different cultural contexts, particularly in developing countries, needs interpretation and specification. The Christian priority towards human dignity and justice necessitates additional safeguards to avoid exploitation or abuse of vulnerable populations due to poverty, lack of education and understanding of scientific issues, lack of technical skills, scarce resources, disease and inability to have access to essential health products and services.

Community consultations might help the process of interpretation to acquire a better knowledge of local culture and involve community representatives in elaborating research projects. In this context, the role of the cultural mediator is essential. The aim is neither to impose foreign ethical standards (in a sort of ethnocentric imperialism or paternalism) nor to adapt to local standards (in a pragmatic relativistic attitude). It is meant to apply generally recognized Christian principles and values and seriously consider the specific culture's conditions and needs with an intercultural and interreligious approach.

Explicitly or implicitly, extra ethically required standards include the following: direct relevance of the clinical trial, equity in enrolment, tailored informed consent, proportionality and compensation for risks and damages and training and assistance to develop "collaborative partnerships."

Informed consent should be tailored to local customs, verifying that it is voluntary and freely given without coercion, incentives or "undue inducements." It may be oral and witnessed for the illiterate, with community leader's permission or family involvement in specific circumstances. In developing countries, participation in a trial could be an incentive to obtain food and primary healthcare and affect their voluntariness and presence of "undue" influence. The socio-economic conditions could push these countries to participate in the research without adequate awareness of the risks.

Another problem consists of some populations' difficulty to grasp the concept of research, which tends to be confused with care and assistance (the so-called therapeutic misconception). Involvement of other persons in formulating informed consent is acceptable only if we can verify the genuine awareness of individual participation (as well as the possibility to withdraw from it) and an absence of direct or indirect external pressure. This awareness should be verified as being personal and cannot be substituted by someone else.

Confidentiality is another issue connected to informed consent. It may be weakened (or obliterated) with the family's possible involvement in the process of granting permission to carry out the research. Some cultures do not have a concept of "privacy." It raises an ethical problem because participation in research may, for some vulnerable populations, carry the stigma of being sick. In such contexts, cultural associations may play a supportive role to help the patients not to be marginalized.

In the Christian perspective, the principles of justice and solidarity require participants to receive appropriate treatments that yield potential benefits. They should, otherwise, be compensated for any harm directly related to participation in research. As an expression of international cooperation and solidarity, healthcare infrastructures are needed to support proper distribution. They guarantee continued access to post-trial benefits and treatment to participants and populations outside the research context of the country where the trial is conducted. It means that protection should be provided through arrangements of mandatory insurance because of possible damages, where the premium is assessed according to the local economic situation. This arrangement could be guaranteed by non-profit and internationally accredited independent organizations, which may monitor this ethical requirement.

An ethical requirement from the Christian perspective is to help developing countries build the capacity to become fuller partners in international research on both scientific and ethical levels, enhancing collaboration and creating an atmosphere of trust and respect. There should be a guarantee of assistance to developing countries during the experimentation without inflicting on them the burden of the "indirect costs" on an already precarious local health system. This collaboration will help them become full partners in international research and stimulate the improvement of the local health system by transferring technical and scientific skills. Involving doctors and representatives of the host country will help monitor compliance with ethical standards and avoid abuse.[13]

Notes

1 Kevin D. O'Rourke and Philip Boyle, *Medical Ethics: Sources of Catholic Teachings* (Washington, DC: Georgetown University Press, 1999); David F. Kelly, Gerard Magill, and Henk ten Have, *Contemporary Catholic Health Care Ethics* (Washington, DC: Georgetown University Press, 2013); Gilbert Meilaender, *Bioethics: A Primer for Christians*, revised ed. (Grand Rapids, MI: W. B. Eerdmans Publishing Co., 2004); Jason T. Eberl (ed.), *Contemporary Controversies in Catholic Bioethics* (Cham, Switzerland: Springer International Publishing AG, 2017); Anthony Fisher, *Catholic Bioethics for a New Millennium* (Cambridge: Cambridge University Press, 2011); Padraig Corkery, *Bioethics and the Catholic Moral Tradition* (Sedona, Arizona: Veritas Publishing, 2011); The National Catholic Bioethics Centre, *A Catholic Guide to Ethical Clinical Research* (Philadelphia, PA: The Catholic Medical Association and the National Catholic Bioethics Centre, 2009); James J. Walter and Thomas A. Shannon, *Contemporary Issues in Bioethics: A Catholic Perspective* (Lanham, MD: Rowman and Littlefield Publishers, 2005).
2 The Catholic Medical Association and National Catholic Bioethics Centre, "Catholic Principles and Guidelines for Clinical Research," *National Catholic Bioethics Quarterly* 7, no. 1 (Spring 2007): 153–165. For the Catholic perspective: Pontifical Council for Pastoral Assistance to Health Care Workers, *Charter for Health Care Workers* (Vatican City: Pontifical Council for Pastoral Assistance to Health Care Workers, 2016), 82–84. See United States Conference of Catholic Bishops, *Ethical and Religious Directives for Catholic Health Care Services* (Washington, DC: United States Conference of Catholic Bishops).
3 John Paul II, "To the Members of the Pontifical Academy for Life," *Address* (February 23, 2003): "The researcher must respect the dignity and nature of the human subject as having the powers of intellect and free will. This fact is the foundation for moral obligations regarding free and informed consent. Generally, both the subject and the researcher must recognize that the subject has moral

obligations under the natural law concerning his or her life. The researcher must always be mindful that subjects have a natural law obligation to care for and conserve their health in a manner proportionate to the specific circumstances. At no time should a researcher attempt to compromise this obligation."

4 "All persons served by Catholic health care have the right and duty to protect and preserve their bodily and functional integrity. The functional integrity of the person may be sacrificed to maintain the health or life of the person when no other morally permissible means is available," see United States Conference of Catholic Bishops, *Ethical and Religious Directives for Catholic Health Care Services*, 29.

5 John Paul II, "To the Participants in a Conference Promoted by the Pontifical Commission for Pastoral Assistance to Health Care Workers," *Address* (November 12, 1987). The Catholic theological and philosophical reflection on the topics in bioethics: Edmund Pellegrino, Daniel C. Thomasma, *The Virtues in Medical Practice* (Oxford: Oxford University Press, 1993); Elio Sgreccia, *Personalist Bioethics: Foundations and Applications* (Philadelphia: National Catholic Bioethics Center, 2012).

6 Laura Palazzani (ed.), "Special Issue on iConsent:—Improving the Guidelines for Informed Consent, Including Vulnerable Populations, under a Gender Perspective," *Rivista di BioDiritto*, Special Issue 1 (2019): 154.

7 Mazur Gregorz, *Informed Consent, Proxy Consent, and Catholic Bioethics: For the Good of the Subject* (Dordrecht: Springer Nature, 2012).

8 *Ibid.*

9 Italian Committee for Bioethics, "Pharmacological Trials on Women," *Opinion* (2008).

10 *Ibid.*, in the personal remarks at the end of the Opinion: "It is ethically acceptable or justifiable from a medical point of view, to force the inclusion of potentially fertile patients in pharmacological clinical trials to use contraceptive methods chosen and imposed by the sponsor and supported by binding clauses from insurance companies, in order to give the necessary economical guarantees to cover possible damages. This request, independently from ethical and religious positions, is not in fact in keeping with the responsible freedom of choice that—within completely personal choices like those regarding married life and the responsibility to procreate—the patient applying to enlist in clinical trials must take on in a personal and independent way, after an exhaustive conversation with the doctor experimenter. In addition, we highlight that contractual imposition from the sponsor of the trials to use contraceptive methods, gives ethical committees, which operate in health institutions regulated by particular rules, some evident difficulties in evaluating and accepting the protocols."

11 Laura Palazzani, "Review of *Clinical Research Involving Pregnant Women* by Françoise Baylis and Angela Ballantyne (eds)," *Theoretical Medicine and Bioethics* 40 (2019): 343–345.

12 John Paul II, "To the Members of the Pontifical Academy of Sciences," *Address* (October 23, 1982).

13 Italian Committee for Bioethics, "Pharmacological Trials in Developing Countries," *Opinion* (2011).

10 Fitting informed consent onto an Islamic moral landscape and within Muslim contexts[1]

Aasim I. Padela

Introduction

Informed consent is a central feature of contemporary medical practice and healthcare research. Scholars have spilled much ink discussing its theoretical foundations, and healthcare professionals have convened many meetings delineating the processes of obtaining informed consent. A casual observer of these discourses may thereby assume that there is no new theoretical ground to break and that informed consent processes are universally practised and globally identical. That observer may be surprised to find that state actors such as the European Union are actively funding research on the ethics and practice of informed consent and that pharmaceutical companies such as GlaxoSmithKline and bioethics institutes such as the UNESCO Chair in Bioethics and Human Rights are actively mapping out religious and cultural dimensions of informed consent. Indeed, there remains much to discover about fulfilling the ideals and meeting the moral ends, of informed consent. This knowledge and research gap is exemplified by scant research at the intersection of the Islamic tradition and informed consent.

Where there is literature, it broadly speaks to the structural, legal and regulatory aspects of informed consent in Muslim countries and thereby bypasses in-depth analyses from within Islamic moral frameworks.[2] Similarly, there are few ethnographic and social scientific studies of the lived experiences of Muslims with informed consent processes and little data on whether such practices met their ethical goals within Muslim healthcare environments.[3] A few scholars have begun to analyse how research ethics is viewed by Islamic jurists[4] and aligns with scriptural values,[5] and this paper aims to build upon these investigations by laying the groundwork for deeper inquiry in theological ethics.

This commentary will consider how the bioethical construct of informed consent fits within an Islamic moral universe. More specifically, I will describe theological concepts that can provide homeomorphic equivalents

DOI: 10.4324/9781003213215-13

for elements of informed consent theory.[6] After this theoretical exposition, I will describe features of Muslim cultures that suggest informed consent procedures and processes need to be re-imagined and culturally adapted. Taking these features into account requires adjustments that will make informed consent processes appear different in Muslim contexts, yet arguably, the adjusted processes will achieve similar ethical ends.

A conception of informed consent

Before diving into Muslim moral contexts, I would like to provide a brief account of informed consent. I readily acknowledge there are multiple origins stories to informed consent and that informed consent practices continue to evolve. I also admit that some aspects of my representation are debatable. However, when analysing my argument, the reader will find this section to be a helpful reference point.

Informed consent is an ethical construct that grows out of the principle of respect for autonomy.[7] The notion of respecting autonomy, in turn, emerges from the view that an essential characteristic of the human person is his/her capacity and ability to make autonomous choices.[8] In this way, respect for autonomy is closely related to respect for persons. This integral human capacity for deliberate choice begets moral duties; one should not infringe upon another's ability to make autonomous choices. Instead, one should facilitate such choice-making in so far as possible. The theoretical roots of informed consent attach themselves to these foundations and are implemented through acts that facilitate the patient's self-regulating decisions. Informed consent doctrine and practice thus seek to maximize the pursuit of self-interest and individual self-regulation.[9] When surrogate decision-makers are involved, the practices are someone altered but still adhere to the same ethos.[10] Notably, the locus of moral concern is the individual, and as they become a right-bearer and all other members of society become morally obligated to not infringe upon those rights.

In a Western context, informed consent is established through regulations and laws that penalize healthcare systems for infringements, and standardized forms assist in seeing the informed consent process through medical care and research. Obviously, to make informed choices, an individual (or a surrogate decision-maker) must be able to understand and process the risks and benefits of the procedure or therapy, thereby meeting the ethical ends of informed consent, that is, autonomous decisions made out of self-interest requires health literacy. Furthermore, theory and practice assume rational actors. Should patients be unable to process the information required to make informed choices, be it due to cognitive deficiencies, acuity of illness or some other reason, then the healthcare team and surrogate decision-makers are morally charged with the duty to protect the patient from the harms of therapy and/or research in so far as possible.[11]

In its ideal form, informed consent theory and practice envision a patient–doctor dyad with reciprocal moral duties and obligations. The patient's ability to make informed decisions needs to be maximized because decision-making is core to being a human person, and the physician is ethically bound to do so and undertakes the responsibility to provide that biomedical data needed to make decisions. This provision of information attends to the "informed" portion of informed consent. To assure consent, the physician attempts to assess whether the patient is being coerced by others to make a certain choice by others. He works with the patient to marginalize such influences if any.

Furthermore, risks and benefits are discussed openly and transparently so that the patient can weigh them, and discussions about a patient's particular values and life goals take place to assess whether the specific choice helps meet them. In this way, the physician acts under Emanuel and Emanuel's interpretative and/or deliberative model for the doctor–patient relationship[12] and informed and voluntarily given consent is enabled. In a structured process, informed consent requires that clinicians (or researchers) provide patients (or research subjects) with sufficient information regarding the medical procedures, potential risks, benefits and alternatives (no matter how remote) so that the individual understands this information and can make a voluntary decision to take the treatment (or enrol in the research study). It further requires physicians (or researchers) to do so in a way that is understandable to the patient (or surrogate decision-makers). Next, informed processing and voluntariness on the part of the patient/ research subject (or surrogate) are accessed, and if satisfactory, then consent is secured and the procedure authorized. As noted earlier, this idealized form of a two-person dyad of a patient and a clinician (or a potential researcher subject and a researcher) often extends to surrogate decision-makers who act on behalf of the patient. Additionally, it can extend to other healthcare team members, such as collaborating physicians and researchers, and encompass family members and important others who are essential to the patient's decision-making process.

As a leading scholar of medical ethics, Mark Siegler argues that moral certitude in the patient–doctor relationship emerges via negotiation between respective worldviews and values.[13] This negotiation results in a "physician-patient accommodation model . . . in which the moral and technical arrangements of a medical encounter are determined mutually, voluntarily, and autonomously"[14] and yields a wilfully chosen, respectful and therapeutic relationship. Informed consent processes are also subject to negotiation whereby patients and doctors accommodate each other's needs and values.

In other words, patients and doctors can negotiate how the process is carried out, who is involved, what sort of information is shared and variations can be ethically justified so long as the dyad is satisfied with the end result of the negotiation.

Islamic moral theology[15] and notions of informed consent

Before venturing into Islamic thought and Muslim practices, several provisos are needed: Islamic morality is pluralistic and Muslim practices are diverse. In addition to their being two dominant sects within Islam, Sunni and Shia, each sect has multiple legal schools and orthodox creedal systems. Thus, finding a singular view on any specific matter of theology or law is challenging. Indeed, moral pluralism is an orthopraxic feature of Islamic thought and enshrined within moral and legal theory.

Additionally, as with any religious tradition, adherents live out their tenets variably. As religious beliefs inform social norms and Muslims turn Islam into a lived tradition, an immense diversity of expression is observed. One need only look to how religious dictates of modesty inform diversity in dress codes and forms of social interaction across the Muslim world to see how different people interpret how to live a religious life. This diversity is increased further when one considers Muslims whose identities are less strongly formed by religious teachings as a Muslim society's norms and practices are constituted by all inhabitants, not simply the most religious amongst them. On top of that, forms of government and state regulations also differ widely across the Muslim world, making chances for uniformity in law and ethics more remote.

On the other hand, pluralism and diversity do not equate with ethical relativism or moral anarchy. Indeed, there must be shared ideas, norms and teaching for there to be something called "Islam." In what follows, I will draw upon shared theological notions and moral teachings to point out homeomorphic equivalencies for informed consent theory within the tradition. Following that, I will describe some cultural features that may require adaptations from following Western informed consent practices to meet the ethical ends of informed consent in the Muslim world.

The notion of moral liability, *taklīf*, provides a theological building block for a Muslim version of informed consent theory. The term symbolizes standing before God in judgement and connotes being morally responsible to God for one's actions. A morally liable person is called a *mukallaf*, and *mukallaf* status signifies that an individual has the requisite cognitive ability to recognize God, evaluate the merits and harms of actions and act wilfully out of self-interest. Therefore, *taklīf* is linked to the maturity of intellect (*'aql*).[16] The minimal intellectual capacity needed to be judged *mukallaf* is the ability to distinguish between beneficial from harmful actions (this state is termed *tamyīz*) while having the maximal faculty leads to the adoption of righteous character (*rushd*).

Closely related to *mukallaf* is the construct of *ahliyyah*, legal capacity.[17] Legal capacity is of two types: *ahliyyah al-wujub* and *ahliyyah al-'ada*. *Aaliyah al-wujūb* is the ability of a human being to acquire rights and obligations, while *ahliyyah al-'ada* is the capacity for execution and performance of duties. This latter capacity is further subdivided into three categories: the capacities related to (i) criminal liability, (ii) civil/financial liability and (iii) liability for acts of ritual worship.[18] While mental/intellectual maturity is a precondition for *taklīf* (and *ahliyyah al-'ada*), because mental faculty has gradations, one can be morally culpable for some acts but not others.

The linkage of *mukallaf* status to the intellectual capacity to distinguish harms and benefits and an ability to execute wilful actions is analogous to the theoretical foundations of informed consent. A person cannot engage in an informed consent process if they do not (i) have the cognitive resources to assess risks and benefits of choosing or are (ii) not free to choose. Being morally accountable for an action in Islam similarly demands that individuals evaluate their options and choose autonomously. Likewise, both informed consent and Islamic law require information to be presented so that a moral choice can be made; the former requiring the biomedical risks, benefits and purposes, and the latter data about the Islamic ethico-legal status of each of the proposed choices. Moreover, just like in informed consent theory, should individuals have diminished mental abilities such that they cannot work through the benefits and harms of choices, surrogate decision-makers come to bear the moral duties of protection. It is important to note that *mukallaf* status is reserved for Muslims within Islamic law, and thus children and non-Muslims are considered to have *mukallaf* potential. The reason for this is that in the religious sense, children are considered to not be morally liable for actions prior to having reached the level of *tamyīz*. Their legal guardians, however, can be liable to provide recompense in this world for harms they commit, for example, paying for stolen items or property damage. Non-Muslims, on the other hand, are obviously not accountable to Islamic law, for they have not chosen Islam as the source of their moral commitments.

Moving from a theoretical space to a more practical one, it appears that Islamic law would support policies and structures that help adults with sufficient intellectual capacity make autonomous choices about medical care and research. *Mukallaf* status appears to provide a homeomorphic equivalency between Islamic thought and informed consent theory such that the prerequisites for moral liability in one system turn out to be the same prerequisites for decision-making in the other. By noting a homeomorphic equivalency,[19] I am not suggesting that the meaning or the function of *taklīf* in the Islamic moral universe shares meaning or function with informed consent procedures in any way. Indeed, they operate not only in different cultural systems; they are constructs that operate at different registers with the former being a theological construct that is reflected into moral law while the latter is an ethical construct reflected within medical practices. Yet, the equivalence is helpful for bridging the values of Islam and contemporary biomedicine.

Another Islamic bioethical argument can be made to support informed consent. According to Islam, every action has moral significance and can bring about reward or retribution in the hereafter. An action that pleases God will be generally rewarded and that which displeases Him will generally be punished. Insights into God's approval or disapproval are found within the Quranic texts and the Prophet's practices. Islamic jurists thus look to these scriptural sources to determine the moral status of actions and place actions into five (or seven) categories from prohibited to obligatory and then map out the moral duties corresponding to each category.[20] For example, a Muslim can be obligated to perform an act, for example, ritual prayer as well as not to perform an act, for example, drinking wine, and sin is carried for shortcomings in either non-performance or performance based on which category the act falls into. Contextual considerations and contingencies are accounted for by allowing exemptions from the normative prohibitions and specifying general rules to individual cases. In light of this, it is important to recognize that seeking medical treatment and participating in research are actions that have Islamic moral significance. Both are considered to be permitted actions but generally non-obligatory, that is, no sin for non-performance.[21] However, at least in the case of seeking healthcare, the moral status of permission can be changed into a moral obligation to pursue treatment when a particular treatment is deemed certainly life-saving or when disability or contagion ensues because of non-treatment.[22] A religious valuation thus depends upon a biomedical assessment of risks, benefits and harms. In other words, to properly assess the moral significance of seeking healthcare (or participating in research), biomedical data regarding the risks, benefits and harms of both non-treatment and potential treatments are necessary.

Hence, religious authorities, patients and surrogate decision-makers all require accurate biomedical data to make moral assessments within Islamic law. Recall that informed consent is built upon the principle of respecting an individual's autonomous decisions that are made voluntarily and also involves evaluating the risks and benefits of various choices. In an Islamic context, every decision has moral significance. For patients (and surrogates) to properly consider both the worldly and afterlife ramifications of seeking healthcare or participating in medical research, accurate information must be conveyed so that the moral agent can process it and make choices without coercion since the individual is morally culpable (to God) for the decisions they make. Hence, informed consent processes aid individuals in living an Islamically moral life.

In closing, Islamic moral theology appears to support informed consent theory and practice. To rightly order one's life towards God's pleasure, that is, act in accordance to Islamic ethics and law, one needs information about biomedical benefits, risks and harms attributable to each choice, one must also have the requisite mental abilities to reason through this data and ultimately be able to make a voluntary choice. Consequently, the biomedical information must be made available in an understandable form, and structures and processes need to be put into place to minimize coercion and undue influence. These ideas grow out of the construct of *taklīf* and the human relationship to God rather than ideas about respecting autonomy or reducing infringements upon humankind's natural rights. One could argue that within an Islamic moral universe, the principle of respect for persons is operative and connects *taklīf* to medical ethics. Certainly, when persons are viewed primarily as moral agents standing before God and the human community as their helpers, communal moral duties are delineated to facilitate individuals being better moral agents. As Sachedina states, Islam legitimizes "individual autonomy within its religiously based collective order by leaving an individual free to negotiate his/her spiritual destiny, while requiring him/her to abide by a communal order that involve[s] . . . a regime of rights and responsibilities"[23] based in Islamic law. Consequently, the individual's exercise of autonomy is somewhat constrained because a communal order of public adherence to Islamic values is privileged. At the same time, the community, and particularly state authorities, become morally responsible for helping its members make righteous choices by providing information and enacting policies and laws that help foster a society that adheres to Islam.

Muslim cultures and informed consent

As medicine has globalized, so has bioethics. Just as medical technology and curricula are patterned after Western academies, bioethics teaching around the world also draws upon ethical principles and moral frameworks first worked out in the "West."[24] It should come as no surprise then that the four-principle Georgetown model of medical ethics is widely taught in Muslim lands and that research and medical practice guidelines in these countries are borrowed from American and European institutions. While there has been increased attention given to formulating medical ethics guidelines based on indigenous Muslim cultural values or based on Islamic law, these efforts are in their infancy and not as yet widespread.[25] Given the scant literature available on informed consent practices in Muslim contexts, these trends suggest that informed consent processes and structures likely mimic implementation models within the United States and Europe. In what follows, I will draw attention to a couple of features of Muslim culture that problematize such consent processes and thereby necessitate revising these procedures to suit Muslim sensibilities and culture.

The first feature that must be considered is that Muslim societies operate out of a communitarian ethos and shared decision-making processes. Many scholars have pointed out that within Muslim societies, the patient–doctor dyad is often not the only locus of decision-making.[26] Instead, an individual in many Muslim societies is better conceived of as a person that "is wedded to social bonds that are inextricable, and [that] these bonds are a vital source of decision-making."[27] People trust their relatives and community members and value interdependence. Therefore, limiting decision-making within person-centric rights can deny the value attached to such relationships.[28] Moreover, as foreshadowed earlier, Islamic law defines rights that an individual has upon their community and relatives. For many Muslims, these need to be accounted for when making medical decisions.[29] However, widening the circle beyond the patient–doctor dyad poses practical and ethical challenges for informed consent processes; how does one know who should be involved and where decisional authority resides? How does one distinguish coercion from acceptable influence by family members and important others? When would "forcing" a patient to act out of self-interest be ethically objectionable? Ethicists have tried to solve these problems through relational and second-order autonomy frameworks, but these fixes appear not to address the issues at hand fully.[30] My colleagues and I have argued elsewhere that, at least theoretically, a culturally tailored version of the principle of respect for persons may offer an alternative ethical guide for clinicians attending to such issues but how such a principle would lead to adaptations in informed consent procedures remains to be worked out.[31]

A second feature of Muslim contexts that needs to be considered is that the culture of communication within many Muslim societies is high context. According to Geert Hofstede, an expert in cross-cultural issues in business, a high-context communication culture is "one in which little has to be said or written because most of the information is either in the physical environment or supposed to be known by the persons involved ... this type of communication is frequent in collectivist cultures."[32] In such cultures, individuals do not expect or desire a great deal of explicit information. Instead, too much information can leave individuals feeling uninformed and can even generate feelings of distrust. By contrast, individuals within low-context cultures rely on mounds of explicit information in written and oral communication and, without such information, are distrustful. In Hofstede's analyses, Arab countries were the most high-context and the United States the most low-context. As Drs. Pablo Rodriguez del Pozo and Joseph Fins, cross-cultural bioethics experts, point out that the doctrine of informed consent is vague on what constitutes adequate information and reasonable disclosure for therapeutic or research purposes.[33] Given that people from high- and low-context societies expect different quanta of information, it appears that what constitutes adequate information might vary from context to context. Indeed, providing too much information in one context can lead patients to distrust clinicians, while too little information leads to the same consequence in another context; the Goldilocks scenario thus arises. As del Pozo and Fins argue, Western standards and structures for informed consent where the doctor shares detailed biomedical data with the patient do not appear to work well in Qatar (an Arab Muslim country).[34] Expert physicians in that society often use family members and nonverbal clues to deliver necessary medical information and effect informed consent. They argue that there "are no objective standards to define the proper mix of verbal and contextual channels to deliver [medical] information, American standards cannot be extrapolated."[35] Allying themselves with Siegler's view on patient–doctor accommodation, they contend that patients and doctors have to construct the moral norm socially and that the notion of self-determination within informed consent doctrine is culturally mediated.[36]

A third feature of Muslim societies that needs to be considered when implementing informed consent processes is how to ground ethics regulations within Islamic law.[37] For example, Saudi laws on research ethics make repeated references to the Shariah as a source of ethical guidance to garner professional support for the statutes.[38] Fogarty-funded research ethics training programs in Jordan similarly seek to support the teaching of the Belmont report by citing Quranic verses that appear to support its principles.[39] Whether or not ethical policies and regulations are built up from the first principles of Islamic law or are based on traditional hermeneutical approaches to scripture does not appear to matter. Rather statements that note that these cohere with Islam are used to legitimize ethical regulations. Indeed, some researchers have pointed out the weak connections between Islamic moral theology and such guidelines.[40] Irrespective of this, the need to, at least rhetorically, attach ethical guidance to Islamic law remains true.[41] Public and professional acceptance depends on such linkages, and ethicists and clinicians seeking to adapt informed consent doctrine and practices need to recognize the thirst for Islamic legitimacy. Research into conceptual analogues and homeomorphic equivalencies between Islamic theology, law and ethics and secular bioethics principles and values will prove fruitful in identifying ways to bridge Islam and contemporary biomedicine authentically.

Conclusion

In this essay, I have outlined how Islamic moral theology appears to support aspects of informed consent doctrine, although the ethical grounding comes from the theological construct of moral liability in front of God, and not from the principle of respect for autonomy. I have also described several features of Muslim culture, namely, its communitarian ethos, high-context communication norms, and need for ethical guidelines to be religiously legitimated, that require amending "western" processes and structures of informed consent for use in Muslim contexts. As the global bioethics community culturally translates and religiously adapts informed consent for implementation in Muslim contexts, informed consent processes may look and feel different in Muslim societies but may serve the same ethical ends.

Notes

1 A version of this paper has been published in as A.I. Padela, "Reflecting and Adapting Informed Consent to fit within an Islamic Moral Landscape and in Muslim Contexts," *Studia Bioethica* 11, no. 2 (2018): 31–39. The paper was also presented, in partial form, at the 6th International Bioethics, Multiculturalism and Religion workshop: Perspectives on Informed Consent. Sponsored by the UNESCO Chair in Bioethics and Human Rights in Rome. Regina Apostolorum University, Rome, Italy in March 2018.
2 Ghiath Alahmad, Mohammad Al-Jumah, and Kris Dierickx, "Review of National Research Ethics Regulations and Guidelines in Middle Eastern Arab Countries," *BMC Medical Ethics* 13, no. 1 (2012); Hany Sleem, Samer S. El-Kamary, and Henry J. Silverman, "Identifying Structures, Processes, Resources and Needs of Research Ethics Committees in Egypt," *BMC Medical Ethics* 11, no. 1 (2010); Mohammad Abdur Rab, et al., "Ethical Practices for Health Research in the Eastern Mediterranean Region of the World Health Organization: A Retrospective Data Analysis," *PLoS One* 3, no. 5 (2008).
3 Ghiath Alahmad, Mohammed Al Jumah, and Kris Dierickx, "Confidentiality, Informed Consent, and Children's Participation in Research Involving Stored Tissue Samples: Interviews with Medical Professionals from the Middle East," *Narrative Inquiry in Bioethics* 5, no. 1 (2015).
4 Ghiath Alahmad and Kris Dierickx, "What Do Islamic Institutional Fatwas Say about Medical and Research Confidentiality and Breach of Confidentiality?," *Developing World Bioethics* 12, no. 2 (2012).
5 Ghiath Alahmad and Kris Dierickx, "Pediatric Research Ethics: Islamic Perspectives," (2015); Hossam E. Fadel, "Ethics of Clinical Research: An Islamic Perspective," *Journal of the Islamic Medical Association of North America* 42, no. 2 (2010).

6 Raimundo Panikkar, *The Intrareligious Dialogue* (New York: Paulist Press, 1999).
7 Marsha Garrison and Carl Schneider, *The Law of Bioethics: Individual Autonomy and Social Regulation*, 2nd ed., American Casebook Series (St. Paul, MN: Thomson/West, 2009); Carl Schneider, *The Practice of Autonomy: Patients, Doctors, and Medical Decisions* (New York: Oxford Unviersity Press, 1998); Tom L. Beauchamp and James F. Childress, "Moral Principles: Respect for Autonomy," in *Principles of Biomedical Ethics* (New York: Oxford University Press, 2009); James F. Childress, "The Place of Autonomy in Bioethics," *The Hastings Center Report* 20, no. 1 (1990); Tom L. Beauchamp and James F. Childress, *Principles of Biomedical Ethics* (Oxford, USA: Oxford University Press, 2001).
8 Schneider, *The Practice of Autonomy: Patients, Doctors, and Medical Decisions*.
9 Beauchamp and Childress, "Moral Principles: Respect for Autonomy."
10 Childress, "The Place of Autonomy in Bioethics."
11 *The Belmont Report: Ethical Principles and Guidelines for the Protection of Human Subjects of Research*, The National Commission for the Protection of Human Subjects of Biomedical and Behavioral Research (1979), http://ohsr.od.nih.gov/guidelines/belmont.html; Larry R. Churchill, "Toward a More Robust Autonomy: Revising the Belmont Report," in *Belmont Revisited: Ethical Principles for Research with Human Subjects*, ed. James F. Childress, Eric M. Meslin, and Harold T. Shapiro (Washington, DC: Georgetown University Press, 2005).
12 E.J. Emanuel and L.L. Emanuel, "Four Models of the Physician-Patient Relationship," *Journal of the American Medical Association* 267, no. 16 (1992).
13 Mark Siegler, "Searching for Moral Certainty in Medicine: A Proposal for a New Model of the Doctor-Patient Encounter," *Bulletin of the New York Academy of Medicine* 57, no. 1 (1981); Mark Siegler, "The Physician Patient Accommodation," *Archives of Internal Medicine* 142, no. 10 (1972).
14 Siegler, "Searching for Moral Certainty in Medicine."
15 I adopt Prof. Mohamed Fadel's usage of the English term moral theology to refer to the Islamic science of *uṣūl al-fiqh*. See M. Fadel, "The True, the Good and the Reasonable: The Theological and Ethical Roots of Public Reason in Islamic Law," *Canadian Journal of Law and Jurisprudence* 21, no. 1 (2008).
16 Imran Ahsan Khan Nyazee, *Islamic Jurisprudence: Usul al-Fiqh* (Islamabad: Islamic Research Institute, 2000); Mohammad Hashim Kamali, *Principles of Islamic Jurisprudence* (Cambridge: Islamic Texts Society, 2003).
17 Oussama Arabi, "Capacity, Legal," in *Encyclopedia of Islam:—Three*, 3rd ed., ed. Kate Fleet, et al., (Leiden, Netherlands: Brill Online, 2013); Nyazee, *Islamic Jurisprudence*.
18 Nyazee, *Islamic Jurisprudence*.
19 Panikkar, *The Intrareligious Dialogue*.
20 Nyazee, *Islamic Jurisprudence*; Kamali, *Principles of Islamic Jurisprudence*; Abdur Rahman I. Doi, *Sharī'ah: The Islamic Law* (London: Ta Ha Publishers, 1984).
21 Omar Qureshi and Aasim I. Padela, "When Must a Patient Seek Healthcare? Bringing the Perspectives of Islamic Jurists and Clinicians into Dialogue," *Zygon* 51, no. 3 (2016). https://doi.org/10.1111/zygo.12273; Mohammed Ghaly, *Islam and Disability: Perspectives in Theology and Jurisprudence* (Abingdon, UK: Routledge, 2010).
22 Qureshi and Padela, "When Must a Patient Seek Healthcare?"
23 Abdulaziz Abdulhussein Sachedina, *Islamic Biomedical Ethics: Principles and Application* (Oxford and New York: Oxford University Press, 2009), 13, www.loc.gov/catdir/toc/ecip0821/2008028322.html.

24 Raymond De Vries and L. Rott, "Bioethics as Missionary Work: The Export of Western Ethics to Developing Countries," in *Bioethics around the Globe*, ed. C. Myser (New York: Oxford University Press, 2011).
25 Mehrunisha Suleman, "Biomedical Research Ethics in the Islamic Context: Reflections on and Challenges for Islamic Bioethics," *Islamic Bioethics: Current Issues and Challenges*, ed. Alireza Bagheri, et al. (Singapore: World Scientific, 2017), 197–228.
26 Aisha Y. Malik, "Physician-Researchers' Experiences of the Consent Process in the Sociocultural Context of a Developing Country," *AJOB Primary Research* 2, no. 3 (2011); Farhat Moazam, "Families, Patients, and Physicians in Medical Decisionmaking: A Pakistani Perspective," *Hastings Center Report* 30, no. 6 (2000).
27 Aasim I. Padela, et al., "[Re]considering Respect for Persons in a Globalizing World," *Developing World Bioethics* (2014), 6. https://doi.org/10.1111/dewb.12045.
28 Malik, "Physician-Researchers' Experiences of the Consent Process"; Padela et al., "[Re]considering Respect for Persons in a Globalizing World."
29 "Fard al-Kifayah," in *The Oxford Dictionary of Islam*, ed. John L. Esposito (Oxford: Oxford University Press, 2003), www.oxfordislamicstudies.com/article/opr/t125/e625#.
30 Catriona Mackenzie and Natalie Stoljar, *Relational Autonomy: Feminist Perspectives on Automony, Agency, and the Social Self* (Oxford: Oxford University Press on Demand, 2000); Anita Ho, "Relational Autonomy or Undue Pressure? Family's Role in Medical Decision-Making," *Scandinavian Journal of Caring Sciences* 22, no. 1 (2008).
31 Padela et al., "[Re]considering Respect for Persons in a Globalizing World"; Malik, "Physician-Researchers' Experiences of the Consent Process."
32 Geert Hofstede, *Cultures and Organizations Software of the Mind* (New York: McGraw-Hill, 2005), 78; Pablo Rodriguez Del Pozo and Joseph J. Fins, "Islam and Informed Consent: Notes from Doha," *Cambridge Quarterly of Healthcare Ethics* 17, no. 3 (2008).
33 Pozo and Fins, "Islam and Informed Consent: Notes from Doha."
34 Ibid.
35 Ibid.
36 Ibid.
37 Suleman, "Biomedical Research Ethics in the Islamic Context."
38 Alahmad, Al-Jumah, and Dierickx, "Review of National Research Ethics."
39 Aceil Al-Khatib and Michael Kalichman, "Responsible Conduct of Human Subjects Research in Islamic Communities," *Science and Engineering Ethics* 25, no. 2 (2017): 463–476.
40 Abbas Rattani and Adnan A. Hyder, "Developing an Islamic Research Ethics Framework," *Journal of Religion and Health* 58 (2019): 74–86. https://doi.org/10.1007/s10943-017-0508-8; Mehrunisha Suleman, "Contributions and Ambiguities in Islamic Research Ethics and Research Conducted in Muslim Contexts: A Thematic Review of the Literature," *Journal of Health & Culture* 1, no. 1 (2016).
41 Suleman, "Contributions and Ambiguities in Islamic Research Ethics."

Index

Aaliyah al-wujūb 120
Africa 14, 32
ahliyyah al-'ada 120
AIDS 68
Analects 74
anatman 64
A4atman al-'ada 66
'aql 119
Aranyakas 90
Aristotle 71, 83
artha 81, 82, 83
Arthasastra 5, 80–83, 89–92; of Kautilya 5, 80, 83
Asia 13, 50
Assisted reproductive technologies (ART) 7
atman 82, 83
Australia 48
Austrian Bioethics Commission 26
autonomy-based 102
autos 59

Back and Curtis 48
Beals 79
Beauchamp, T.L. 59, 60, 76
Beecher, K.H. 45
Belmont Report 12, 45, 84, 124
beneficence 106
Benson, P. 66
Bhagavad Gita 82
brahmacharya 81
Brahman 82, 83, 89, 90; *Brahmin* 81, 89
Brahma Sutras 82
Brandt, K. 79
breastfeeding 111–112

Brody, H. 46, 47
Buddhism 2, 4, 59, 63–64, 82, 83, 89

Catholic 106, 109, 111
Catholic Medical Association 105
chaturashramas 81
children 18–23, 108, 109, 112; emancipated minors 27
Childress, F. 59, 60, 76
China 50, 62, 64, 68; Chinese 62, 67, 68, 73
Christian 2, 6, 109–112
citta-bhāvana 66
coercion 113
cognitivism 105
collectivism 62
communal (autonomy) 12, 122
communitarianism 38, 98, 123
confidentiality 113
Confucius 73; Confucian 2, 4, 71–73, 76
conscience 4, 72, 107
cosmopolitan community 63
Council for International Organization of Medical Sciences (CIOSM) 1, 26, 35, 36
Crawford 79
creation 6, 105

dao 73; *dadao* 15
de 71
Declaration of Helsinki 1, 18, 59
developing countries 112
dharma 5, 16, 81–83; *dharma sastric* 89

Index

din 98
Dworkin, G. 47

EMA 25
Emanuel and Emanuel 46, 118
embryo *see* foetus
epagoge 90
equality 108
ethical research committees 16
ethnic minorities 14, 16, 22, 49
eudaimonia 71
Europe 48, 122, 123; European Union (EU) 1, 22
European Group on Ethics in Science and New Technologies 35
Evans, J. 46

familism 62, 75, 76
finalism 105
Fins, J. 124, 126
foetus 6, 111–112
Food and Drug Administration (FDA) 87
free will 4, 47, 64

Garfield, J.L. 66
Georgetown University 122
Goldilocks 124
grihastha 81–83
gui 71
guru 82
Gypsy 13, 50

halakha 97, 98, 101, 102
halal 15
hassid shoteh 98
hassidut 98
he 71
hekesh 97
Helsinki Convention 102
Hindu 16, 80, 83; Hinduism 2, 5, 6, 80, 83
Hippocratic Oath 73
HIV *see* AIDS
Hofstede, G. 123, 124
homeless 112
homeomorphic equivalencies 116, 119, 124
Horizon 2020 i-Consent 1–3
HPV 12

human experimentation 81
Hume, D. 65, 77

immigrants 112
incapacitated 106, 108
India 5, 81; Constitution of 80
individualism 62
Institute of Medicine 24
Institutional Review Board 37
International Bioethics, Multiculturalism and Religion Workshop 2
International Bioethics Committee (IBC) 22, 28
International Conference on Harmonisation of Technical Requirements for Reg istration of Pharmaceuticals for Human Use (ICH) 25
International Covenant on Civil and Political Rights (ICCPR) 79, 80
International Covenant on Economic, Social and Cultural Rights 79
Islam 2, 7, 13, 50, 80, 116, 120, 122, 124
Israel 102, 103
Italian National Bioethics Committee 14

Jain 82, 89
Jakobovitz, I. 100
Japan 13, 50, 64
Jesus 6, 107
Jewish 97, 100; Judaism 2, 5–7
Jonas, H. 99

kama 81–83
karma 66, 82, 83
kashrut 103
Kautilya 6
Kenya 32
kosher 15
Kshatriyas 81

li 71
Locke, J. 85
London 100
low-context cultures 124

Mantra 89
maslahat al-ummah 16

Index

meningitis 12
Michelangelo 52
Middle East 13, 50
Milinda 64
military 112
minors *see* children
moksha 81–83, 90
moksha dharma 82, 92
moral individualism 63
moral liability 7, 119
mukallaf 119, 120
Muslim 7, 82, 116, 117, 119, 123–125
mystical 32

Nagasena 64, 65
National Catholic Bioethics Center 105
Navaho 13
Netherlands 15
New England Journal of Medicine 45
Nigeria 14
Nikhilananda 90
nomos 59
non-maleficence 106
Nuffield Council on Bioethics 20, 24
Nuremberg code 1, 44, 59, 79, 84

Organization of Revenue Collection 90
Oviedo Convention 1

paediatric *see* children
paramarthasa 64
paternalism 45, 74, 106
patient and public involvement (PPI) 33
patient-centered 11
Patient Self-determination Act 45
Persampieri, L. 13
pluralism 119
Politics 83
Pope Pius XII 84, 85
pregnant 111–112
principle of freedom and responsibility 105
principle of precaution 108
principlism 45, 46; *Principle of Biomedical Ethics* 59
prisoners 112
privacy 3, 6, 11, 12, 113
Prophet (Mohammed) 121
Protestant 106

psychological 3, 18, 21, 65–66, 84
puruṣartha 81

Qatar 124
qi 74
Quran 121, 124

randomization 33
Rawls, J. 4, 72
relational autonomy 2–3, 12–14, 38–39, 44, 52, 66
relativism 113, 119
ren 72, 73, 74; *renshu* 73; *renzheng* 73
Report on Traditional Medicine Systems and their Ethical Implications 22
Rodriguez del Pozo, P. 124, 126
RSV 12
rūpa 64
rushd 120

sabbath 98
Sachedina 122
sadhana 82
samadhi 82
sa2adh 64
samsara 82
sa2saran 64
samvrtisat 64
sannyasa 81, 83; *sannyasin* 84, 90
Sanskrit 80, 81, 86
Sebring 79
secular bioethics 124
setsumei to doi 62
Sharia(h) 7, 124
shastras 81
Shudras 81
Siegler, M. 118, 124
Sikhism 86
skandhas 64, 65
solidarity 98
supererogatory 98
supernatural approach 32
surrogate 107, 117
sutras 81
Szasz and Hollander 44, 45

taklīf 7, 119–122
Talmud 97

tamyīz 120
therapeutic hope 110
therapeutic misconception 88, 113
therapeutic obstinacy 110
therapeutic principle 105
therapeutic responsibility 106
Torah 97, 98

unemployed 112
UNESCO Chair in Bioethics and Human Rights 2, 116
UNESCO Declaration of Bioethics and Human Rights 1, 2, 59–61, 63, 116
UNESCO International Bioethics Committee (IBC) 12, 22, 27, 28
United Kingdom (UK) 32
United Nations (UN) 79
United States (USA/US) 13, 22, 46, 48, 50, 86, 88, 122–124
Universal Declaration of Human Rights 1
Universal Declaration on the Human Genome and Human Rights 1
Upanishads 82, 90
upāya 68

vaishyas 81
vanaprastha 81, 82, 90
varṇas 82

Veda 64, 80, 82, 83, 89–91; *Atharva Veda* 89; *Rigveda* 82, 89; *Samaveda* 82, 89, 93; *Vedic Brahmin* 84; *Vedic Samhitas* 82
vijñāna 64
virtue 4, 5, 8, 71–77, 81
vulnerability 8, 11, 12, 14, 15, 18, 19, 23, 24, 27, 31–33, 68, 103, 105, 106, 108, 109, 113

Waldenberg, R. 100, 101
Western 2, 4, 8, 62, 81, 116, 117, 122, 124; non-Western 11
World Health Organization (WHO) 14, 31, 34
World Medical Association 1, 18
World War II 44, 79

xiao 71
xiaodao 15
xin 71

Yajurveda 82, 89
yang 74
yi 71, 72
yin 74

zhi 71
zhishan 71, 72
Zimra, B.D. 97–99

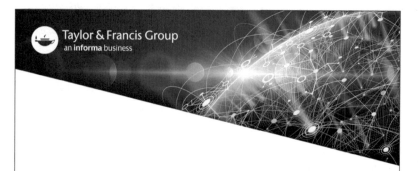